"Hey! It's 2010 and it's about time ̶ ̶
teach men how to love them too..
ladies know what they're talking about so men, listen up!
Joni and Esther were two of my favorite guests ever and
the book is amazing! I can't wait to have them back!"
~Tiffany Granath, Playboy Radio Host of Afternoon
Advice

"In this wonderful book, Esther and Dr. Joni not only tell us
how to keep sex fun, but also show us that intimacy goes
beyond genders. Whether you're straight, lesbian, gay, or
bisexual, what makes the intimate connection is caring,
attentiveness, and the will to keep each other's passion
alive. We may first be attracted to our partner's physique,
but attentiveness to each other's needs and pleasures is
the secret ingredient to *Love Her Right*. I recommend it for
men and women who want to keep their passion alive."
~Jim Bierman, PhD, author of *Of Sound Mind
to Marry; A Reality Check from the marriage
Counselor for Pre-Weds*

"Reading this book is like being a fly on the wall in a trance
at the back and forth banter between two connected
Women. Their real insights and loving souls are nectar from
the Gods for Men who deserve insider information about
how Women work. If you want to know how a car works,
ask a mechanic. If you want to know how Women work,
read this book!"
~Corey Donaldson, author of *Don't You
Dare Get Divorced Until You Read This!*
www.TheFreedomAcademy.com

"As an expert on romance, I have read my share of books on the topics of love, relationships and sex, but Dr. Joni's and Esther's *Love Her Right* absolutely takes the proverbial cake for a number of reasons:

- Their book explains the importance of a healthy relationship for good sex.

- It's written in a voice men can understand easily.

- The authors are funny, bawdy, and straight-forward, holding nothing back.

- The point of view (lesbians helping heterosexual men) is fresh and makes sense.

- Not only is it filled with terrific comprehensive information, but the reader is never bored, because it also includes tips, lists, personal anecdotes, couples activities, and quizzes.

Love Her Right is easily one of the best, all-in-one-place books I have read for men who plan to use their penis for more than just urination."

~Leon Scott Baxter, "America's Romance Guru" and author of *A Labor With Love* and *Out of the Doghouse* (CouplesCommittedToLove.com)

"With uncomplicated conversation, Dr. Joni and Esther bring healthy honor and respect to romantic, sexual love in relationship. Mars and Venus will be much happier with each other after reading this book."

> ~Barbara J. Semple, bestselling author of *Instant Healing – Accessing Creative Intelligence for Healing Body and Soul*

"To say that *Love Her Right: The Married Man's Guide to Lesbian Secrets for Great Sex!* is comprehensive is an understatement. It is a mixture of cook book, apothecary, instruction manual, and support group. The authors' encouragement of men, the book's primary audience, is generous and heartfelt, lacking even the slightest hint of male bashing. Instead, it offers the authors' knowledge as women and as spouses to empower men to be the great lovers most aspire to be."

> ~Dr. Beth Erickson, host of "Relationships 101" on www.webtalkradio.net, author of *Marriage Isn't for Sissies: 7 Simple Keys to Unlocking the Best Part of Your Life*

"At last, the missing manual for your woman's body, as well as her heart and soul. Dr. Joni and Esther show you how to shake up a chemical cocktail in order to connect more deeply on every level. You get the science, you get the vocabulary, and you get the, um, hands-on tips. Learn to be her intimate, erotic friend – and love the benefits!"

> ~Susan Kuchinskas, author of *The Chemistry of Connection*

Love Her Right

The Married Man's Guide
to Lesbian Secrets for Great Sex!

Dr. JONI FRATER &
ESTHER LASTIQUE

ISBN: 1-4392-6065-6
ISBN-13: 9781439260654
Library of Congress Control Number: 2009910326

Dedication:

We dedicate this book to all of the couples who are willing to live their lives with more passion and accept that how we choose to love has no boundaries or limitations. Your courage to take responsibility to redefine your relationship and reach for the ultimate path to self and couple awareness is inspirational. You are bringing positive energy to the world, instilling acceptance and gratitude for the beauty of love. What we can accomplish together as an army of Love Warriors is necessary and unstoppable. We honor you and thank you for joining our quest.

Acknowledgments

There are so many people to thank that the list could go on for the length of this book. This project began as a glimmer of hope, and there were several special people who inspired us to take ourselves on and live up to the vision that began to unfold.

On the home front, we need to thank the members of our team, without which *Love Her Right* would have been sorely lacking. Our Web designer extraordinaire Chuck W. Nelson continues to mesmerize us with his talent and ingenuity, and we have lovingly knighted him "our son." The design team of Paul Kane, Heather Buchanan, Adan Bravo, and Akeim Ford made *Love Her Right* beautiful. The staff at Matrix Media: Brad, Lorna, Brian, and Mary Lou, who gave us the opportunity to create the Love Her Right radio show on webtalkradio.net will always hold a special place in our hearts, and have our thanks.

We are eternally grateful to T. Harv Eker and the entire training staff at Peak Potentials, who lit our fire and kept it burning. We are also infinitely grateful for all of our brilliant mentors, including Jack Canfield, Alex Mandossian, Peggy McColl, Alex Carroll, Joel and Heidi Roberts, John Kehoe, Topher Morrison, Joe Vitale, and so many others who have given us the tools necessary to make *Love Her Right* possible. They pushed us out of the nest and gave us the wings to fly.

The litany of authors, product specialists, and contributors who made Love Her Right Radio take flight have also provided invaluable resource material and insight into the study of love and human sexuality. You also discovered where information was lacking or, worse, incorrect and misleading, and you rose to the challenge to solve the problem. We have followed in your footsteps, and we honor this path that you have blazed by making inroads of our own. For all of you we are grateful.

We are particularly grateful to Bobby O'Neal of Synchrohearts who gave his heart and support to our project. We also need to thank Michele at Eldorado for her continued support and dedication to customer service.

To the editorial, design, marketing, and sales team at BookSurge/Create Space: you rock! Without your talent and guidance, we would still be fumbling around the Internet, searching for the right team. *Love Her Right* is a reflection of all that you are capable of, and we thank you.

And as always, we have saved the best for last. Our loving family and friends have provided us with more than love and support: you have been our sounding boards, our confidantes, our most loyal fans, our researchers, and our biggest cheerleaders.

Dr. Joni To my beloved family: To me, words that go unexpressed are lost opportunities. Words that go into print will become the legacy that you have given to me. I would like to pass this legacy on to all who read this book. Make no mistake about it. It is my good fortune to be able to thank my parents for always telling me that I can be anything that I want to become. This stood true through many good, and some trying times. You have been the source of my strength, sensitivity, tenacity, my inspiration and my love. I am the person that I am because of you and am eternally grateful for our having a strong, loving family.

To my Esther: You are my love, my best friend and my soul mate. The Hebrew phrase: "I am my beloved's and

Acknowledgments

my beloved is mine" is the thought that I wake up to every day that we have together. I am blessed and grateful for the love that we share and hope to inspire others to reach for this goal. Our love soars on heavenly wings!

Esther To my beloved family: There really are no words to express the depth of love and gratitude that I have for all that you are and all that you have helped me to become. Mom and Dad, the strength of character and of the love you share, through all of life's joys and challenges, has been an inspiration to me and has led me to this place of being able to honor your example with my own. It is also in loving memory of my maternal grandparents that I silently dedicate this book: your love brought you across a great ocean, leaving behind all of the pain you knew to give birth to a new family. My gratitude for your strength, love, and tenacity transcends time and space.

To my beautiful Joni: You are my heart, my joy, and the world looks brighter and more colorful because you are in it with me. You are my basheret and I am yours, and I relish every day we get to spend together—you take my breath away and fill me with gratitude for a Higher Power that had so much love for me that we were brought together by that Divine Wisdom.

Our siblings Sharon, Craig, and Shelley, your humor, devotion, and support warm our hearts on a daily basis. Our friends, the extended family of our creation, are too numerous to name but we will try: Paul and Dan, Susan, Janis and Ellen, Tom and James, Steve, Jon, and Steven and Russell, your humor, antics and constant unwavering support of our crazy project kept us laughing. And to Suzanne and Paul, Shana and Kevin, Beth and Alan, Judith and Jason, Sherry and Clyde, and Beverly and Gordon: the love you share is an inspiration to us and to everyone you touch. You are our true Love Warriors, and we salute you. And for our furry babies Gypsy and Rocky, we are in deep gratitude for your daily lessons in unconditional love, and wet sloppy kisses.

Without all of you, we would never have had the faith and tenacity to see this project to the end. We love you and we stand in a place of overwhelming gratitude.

Table of Contents

Introduction

So I bet you're sitting there wondering what possessed you to purchase this book. Come on, you're a guy that's in a committed relationship, with a woman you care for, and you have a sexual relationship. You've had your share of experiences, and you're probably no stranger to variety and how partners differ. Now all this may be true, but something about this book appealed to you. Be honest—you're curious. I mean, aren't all red-blooded guys curious, almost voyeuristically so, about lesbians? What exactly do they do, and how do they do it? Well, we are going to assume your answer is an enthusiastic yes, or you wouldn't be reading this right now.

Why don't we start with who we are and how we got here. We are Dr. Joni Frater and Esther Lastique, and we are a committed couple for seven years now. Six years ago, we decided to take the plunge and were married on a beach in the Caribbean surrounded by family and friends, copious amounts of flowers, and champagne. One of the reasons we feel that our relationship has weathered time and many hardships, including illness, job changes, deaths in both families, and relocation, is that we always remember two secrets: laughter and passion.

Let us tell you why we chose to write this book. As a couple, we are very "out," meaning we don't hide who we are in public. We are affectionate and comfortable enough with our sexuality that we don't mind the occasional question or two. Many of our friends, relatives, and basically everyone we meet have been telling us that while their sex lives are OK, there seems to be something missing, like a little spark has gone out. This holds true for all relationships we encounter, gay and straight alike. We've heard many of these stories from a lot of couples who have been married for a while and might want to spice things up a bit. We discovered in our research that while there is a vast array of relationship advice books on the market, few of them speak directly to men, and of those few, almost none of them are written by women. Many men today have serious questions about sexuality and rejuvenating their relationships, with few answers that really work for them and their partners. Watching loved ones go through the pain of breakups and divorce, we decided that we have something to offer that men might relate to, and *Love Her Right* began to take shape.

Over the years, we have had a few intriguing experiences that were all similar, revolving around one topic: how can straight men learn (or be taught) to please a woman sexually like a lesbian does. What we have found incredible is the rash of comments from our heterosexual friends that are astounding. Here are a few examples:

- *The next time I'm single (i.e., after he's dead or I've given up), I'm going to be with a woman—men just don't get it. (This has been the most popular comment from women over forty who have never before had a sexual experience with a woman.)*

- *Can you give my husband/boyfriend a few tips? He has no clue about female anatomy and thinks oral sex is only something I do to him.*

Introduction

- *Hey, girls, you two must be really sexy. Can I join in or just watch? You know my last wife/girlfriend left me for a woman. Maybe I could use a few pointers. (Our usual response to this is "Not all of us are bisexual" or a flat "Keep dreaming" seems to work just fine.)*

The fact that these comments have also happened at an amazing array of family functions, vacations, and generally everywhere we go (especially if alcohol is present) made us think about the state of affairs of heterosexual relationships. In reality, you guys have it rough. Nearly 70 percent of all marriages don't make it, and finding a new partner in this day and age is an intimidating proposition to say the least. The three biggest reasons relationships dissolve include money, lack of communication, and sexual incompatibilities. Now the money thing is big, but if the sex and communication are lousy, there is no hope. Good sex makes all the other shortcomings seem manageable, and great sex may forgive a lot of transgressions. **There is no faster, easier, or cheaper way to save your relationship, enhance it, or bring it to new heights than improving your sexual connection**. That is why you are reading this right now: you know this is true, and you hope that we can help.

Here's the truth: no one knows a woman's body better than a woman. Since we possess the same anatomy and have an understanding of our different intimate parts and how they work, we already possess an almost unfair advantage. What's more, as lesbians, we are the same emotional creatures as our partners, so we understand a woman's emotional needs from a personal level too. We understand at a core level what turns a woman on emotionally, physically, and sexually. One of the biggest hurdles in any relationship is mastering the art of communication; discovering the basic differences in how men and women communicate can provide guidance as to how to overcome most of life's difficulties. Our goal is to help men and women bridge this gap in order to overcome basic differences in terms of how each thinks and how it translates to individual sexual needs.

When you look at it this way, you might worry that the secrets you need are locked away in a world that you are not a part of. Some people would view us as an unlikely source of information for heterosexual relationships. But, no worries, my friend. For the first time, we are prepared to reveal our secrets to you about everything from anatomy to technique and from romance to seduction.

We have interviewed dozens of authors on our radio show about sex and sexuality, communication, and conflict resolution in relationships. In our research, we have read numerous books about each of the topics covered in this book from many disciplines and cultures. Our curiosity has led us on a quest to uncover the truths that have been suppressed, misconstrued, or hidden that can lead you to a happier, more passionate life.

Why are we sharing this information? Well, it's simple really. As a couple, we know that we are blessed. The type of relationship we have (rich in laughter, friendship, and passion) is the envy of friends and strangers alike, both gay and straight. We understand that what we've got is not common, and that saddens us both. Our wish is that every couple gets the opportunity to create the incredible level of love we share. And our dream is to help couples repair their prior wounds and overcome them in order to make their life together a profound declaration of the joy they possess. What is life without passion? It's like living a shell of a life—hollow, colorless, with no flavor or depth. We believe that life should be overflowing with moments of joy and passion, connections with loved ones, and a tender loving legacy to leave when our time here is done.

Introduction

What could be more important than showing people easy ways to bring more passion into their lives? Love and Passion are the greatest gifts available to us and the greatest gifts you can share with another person. And they're free! Imagine the way our world would change if more of us were happy, living lives full of passion. Wouldn't it be transforming to be a part of raising a generation of kids who think it's cool that Mom and Dad hold hands, kiss, or giggle late at night when their bedroom door is locked? Raising children with positive examples of a happy, healthy, romantic relationship, made up of two fulfilled sexual beings, is a gift that has no price tag. Show them that marriage is a wonderful thing, that's rich in laughter and passion, not disposable like everything else in this culture. Do that, and you'll be able to share the same example of love and passion when the grandkids come over too!

Our point is this: If you want to have better sex than ever before, the best advice we can give is to become your woman's fantasy lover, partner, and intimate friend. How? Well, let's get started!

One Book, Two Voices

We should probably also mention that writing this together was no small feat, since we possess separate and powerful personalities. Dr. Joni is the kinder and gentler one of the two of us. Esther is the "lipstick lesbian"—always fashionably dressed, always feminine, and, for better or worse, always opinionated. While we love each other fiercely, we occasionally disagree, and there are topics mentioned in this book that stirred up differences of opinion between us. To address that to your best advantage, we decided to put in sidebars where we each may have more insights to express, or a divergence of thoughts that might be useful for you so that you may hear two women's different opinions. We also thought this banter might help our readers get to know us and appreciate that although couples may disagree, it doesn't mean they don't love each other. In fact, we feel that passionate discussions are a great way to begin experiencing more passion in your relationship.

How to read this book

While we appreciate that many of you reading this book are going to jump directly to the section on sex and technique, please consider that in the laying out of this book, there was a method to our madness. We decided to create a roadmap with the format, which is especially helpful for those of you experiencing bumps in the road in your relationship. If it has been awhile since you and your partner have been intimate, joyful, or communicating well, please try to read this book our way.

- Part 1 "What Brings Us Together and What Keeps Us Apart" will give you insights into how to improve communication between you and how to build a loving bridge back to one another.

- Part 2 "Applying What You Have Learned So Far" is an opportunity to apply the information you have gathered so far, by spending more time together and having more fun. This means you are working your way back to a place of intimacy.

- Part 3 "How Do Women Work—Really" gives you an inside track to how women work mentally, emotionally, and physically, which sheds light on what makes her tick.

Introduction

- Part 4 "Technique, Timing, and Touch: The Art of Making Love to Your Woman" is what everyone wants to read! From kissing and massage to seduction and sexual techniques, this information will turn your sex life red hot today and tomorrow.

- Part 5 "Life Happens—How to Keep it Sexy" talks about the curve balls life and time can throw at us and how to keep relationships passionate and loving in spite of them.

Reading the book in the order it was created is beneficial because the sections build upon each other. If you are feeling stuck in a rut in your relationship, you may find that this can serve as the path back to your beautiful mate. Take this journey together: read parts of this book as a team, and do the exercises. The information you will gather about yourself and your partner will transform your relationship and your sex life.

For those of you reading this book cover to cover, you will notice we repeat ourselves, especially where health concerns apply. This is intentional, since we figured that many of you are skimming this book, looking for the highlights. Please know that when we repeat something, it's important enough for you to take notice!

Once you have read the book and begun applying the principles, reread chapter 1 and consider taking our Love Warrior Challenge. Discuss it with your partner, visit our Web site at www.LoveHerRight.com, and decide to make passion a priority in your relationship and life. While the sex will be fun and exciting, the transformation your relationship will experience will be life altering. Join us on this journey to deeper levels of love, intimacy, and passion, and maybe we can change the world together—one couple at a time.

"Life without love is a tree without blossom and fruit."

–Kahlil Gibran, poet

CHAPTER I.
Our Challenge to You: Become A Love Warrior

When we started the Love Her Right project, our books were originally released in electronic form, for easy download from our Web site. We had a dream that took years to take shape—a fully integrated online adult site that had the answers people, men in particular, were looking for about how to be better lovers and better partners to the women in their lives. We dreamt of the ability to provide everything people would need to live their lives more passionately, from educational materials to gifts and a wide assortment of products for kicking the sexy meter up a notch, to one day offering seminars and partnering with other experts in this growing field of relationship specialists and sexology. (We are both believers in education, and we have done many seminars together on several topics that have taught us more about life, love, money, and business than all our years of school—including higher education.)

Quite unexpectedly, we were given the opportunity to host our own Internet-based talk radio show, and we jumped on it. We now had the opportunity, and the platform, to connect with other experts in the field and expand our vision of what Love Her Right could look like. We instituted a cool spot on our home Web site, www.LoveHerRight. com, where people could "Ask Dr. Joni and Esther" any questions they had, and suddenly the floodgates opened, especially after we were interviewed on *Playboy's* XM/

Sirius Radio Station. As our dream blossomed, we began to feel that our e-books, while informative and helpful, needed to be expanded and more information needed to be covered, considering the content of the questions that poured in from our audiences. You are embarking upon the result—a new and improved handheld version of *Love Her Right: The Married Man's Guide to Lesbian Secrets for Great Sex!*

As we were wrapping our heads around sitting down to write this book yet again, we both began visiting bookstores and picking up additional pieces of our research puzzle. We have a confession to make: we are both bookstore junkies. While we love the Internet and the potential for research at our fingertips, we are both suckers for paper and ink and the glory of sitting in the sun with a good book and a cocktail.

It was this love of all things published that caused Esther to wander into a Borders bookstore one afternoon at JFK International Airport, en route back to Florida after a visit with her parents. As usual, she found herself in the relationship and sex/self-improvement section, which is where she found what has become a pivotal book for our entire project. Written by Doug Brown, *Just Do It – How One Couple Turned Off the TV and Turned On Their Sex Lives for 101 Days (No Excuses!)* is the eloquent story of how one couple committed to having sex for 101 consecutive days with two small children and two growing careers to manage. After fourteen years of marriage, Doug and Annie Brown made the commitment to reignite their relationship and put their sexual connection on the front burner of life. Here's the best part: they did it with no small amount of difficulty. They managed to win this marathon of their own creation, in spite of illnesses (his and child based), work stress, hectic schedules, exhaustion, and endless child-rearing responsibilities.

Our Challenge to You: Become A Love Warrior

Reading Doug's book shifted our perspective on our project. There is much to be said for quality *and* quantity of lovemaking. When we connect as a couple on a passionate level, it brings us closer together, and reaffirms our commitment to the love we share. But when you make a bold commitment to having that sexual connection daily for an extended period of time, something magical happens. Your whole life begins to take on a new vibration; passion has now electrically charged your entire existence. Colors are brighter, flavors are more intense, senses are heightened, and the world seems like a friendlier place. We don't think it's our imagination. When relationships begin and the passion of new love takes over, it's like your whole life is run by your hormones. You feel sexy, and that feels awesome. What Doug and Annie experienced is that this journey of 101 days of sex brought that same kind of palpable electricity back into their world, and their relationship, after fourteen years of being together. It is our belief that any couple can revisit the tantalizing period of sexual discovery, no matter how long you have been together. The advantage of taking this journey now is that you know each other, and knowing what you know now gives you the opportunity to delve deeper into what turns each of you on today and what will turn you on tomorrow.

So here it is...what one little sojourn into an airport bookstore has born. We have a challenge for you. No matter where your relationship is right now—if things are good but could use a little excitement or if you need to make some serious repairs—it is time to make the choice.

"How you do anything is how you do everything."

–T. Harv Eker, founder of Peak Potentials &
Author of *Secrets of the Millionaire Mind*

We are throwing down a challenge to each of our readers—decide today to become Love Warriors. Sit down with your partner and read this book together or take turns reading it. While it's written for you, it's important for her to see what kind of lessons you're learning. And make a choice. Choose to make your relationship—your love—your most important priority, and do that by making a commitment to making a daily sexual connection. Together, you get to decide what that is for you—mandatory intercourse as did Annie and Doug, mutual orgasms, or whatever agreed-upon ground rules work for you. Once you set those ground rules, they are sacred. Every day, for the duration you choose, is a mandatory meeting of libidos that should regularly take you to new heights of passion and connection. We understand that everyone does not have the tenacity or confidence to commit to 101 days of daily sex, so we have developed a few alternatives. Decide together what time span might work for you: 14 days, 30 days, 50 days, 75 days, or the big kahuna of 101 days.

Go to www.LoveHerRight.com, log in to "Become a Love Warrior," and pick the time span of the challenge you are willing to take on. Unlike Doug and Annie, you now have an incredible resource of information, education, and camaraderie to support you through your journey. We are in the process of creating the Love Her Right Member Site, where there will be regular articles, sex tips, featured products and reviews, instructional videos and podcasts, and interviews with successful couples who are fellow Love Warriors. You also have the power to enter in all of your personal information, like both of your e-mail addresses, lingerie sizes, favorite colors, anniversary and birthdays, and so on. This gives us the opportunity to e-mail you reminders that a special day is coming, so we can help you remember. You will also have the convenience of one-stop shopping at our store Web site, www. LoveHerRightStore.com, where you will find everything you need for seduction, passion, and researching new and adventurous sexual techniques.

We are continuously adding products to the store site to help you with your challenge, and for you guys who love to point, click, buy, and be done, we are going to set up Love Warrior Packages that are perfect for each level of the challenge, no matter which one you pick. Of course, you'll also find lots of guidance from how to choose a sex toy to how to determine your wife's lingerie size without asking her. As members, you will be privy to special discounts on every purchase made in preparation for and during your challenge with your own priority code, and special offers for new products before anyone else gets to sample them. Our intention is to also be able to provide you with access to everything you need to make your seduction be complete; so, as we write this, we are looking for more companies to affiliate with, which you will be able to find right on the Member Site. There will always be more in store because we are constantly coming up with new ways to maximize your Love Her Right experience.

So the choice is yours. If your relationship could use a little bit of fire, or a gallon of gasoline, take on our challenge and become Love Warriors. You've got nothing to lose and a new sexy passionate existence to gain. Revitalize your relationship and watch what happens to the rest of your world. We believe that when you show the courage to put love and passion into the Universe, the Universe responds in kind. Like attracts like, so watch out—more passion is going to flow into your life from unexpected directions. You will be happier with yourself, with your partner, and with the world around you. If you need inspiration before you decide, please read Doug Brown's *Just Do It*. There is no better path than the one less traveled, but reading someone else's account of the bumps in the road you might someday encounter along the way can be comforting and, at times, hilarious. It's rare that a book changes our lives, especially in an era where printed material may soon become a thing of the past. We hope to be for you what Doug and Annie were for us: conspiratorial comrades-in-arms in a plot to make this world a more loving and passionate place, one couple at a time.

"Do you want me to tell you something really subversive?
Love is everything it's cracked up to
be. That's why people are so
cynical about it… It really is worth fighting for,
being brave for, risking everything for. And the
trouble is, if you don't risk everything,
you risk even more."

—Erica Jong, writer and poet

Part One: What Keeps Us Apart and What Brings Us Together

"Love me without fear
Trust me without questioning
Need me without demanding
Want me without restrictions
Accept me without change
Desire me without inhibitions
For a love so free...
Will never fly away."

–Dick Sutphen, writer

CHAPTER 2.
Relight Her Fire For A New Beginning

If we told you this chapter was about communication, we know you would be rolling your eyes already. Don't freak out. We're not suggesting that you process every feeling on the couch in front of the six o'clock news or cry at every Hallmark commercial. Just understand that men and women really are completely different creatures. Women are more emotionally structured—they feel more and make choices based on emotional responses. Guys make decisions based on trying to fix problems. We're here to help you bridge that gap. (That Mars and Venus thing is really true!)

Communication is the key if you want to know how she is feeling. **DON'T GUESS!** Ask her. It's not difficult. Practice with little things. "How was your day, dear?" works well, but here's the secret—you have to **listen intently** to the answer to the question you ask, not just hear it, and look her in the eyes while you are asking and listening. Asking is only part of the deal.

Showing that you care about the answer is what will make all the difference to her. What do we mean? Well, say your wife begins telling you about her day—please don't tune out. When she's done telling you that she accomplished more in one hectic day than the Senate does in a week, you chime in with the one thing she forgot to do like picking up your dry cleaning. You could approach it in an entirely new way: "Wow, honey, it sounds like you got a lot done today. All I did was go to work and come home. Can I help take a few things off your plate for tomorrow? I can pick up the dry cleaning if you like." Chances are you go right past it on your way to work or on your way home. Of course, if you don't know where the dry cleaner is located, don't worry; their address is probably on the claim ticket.

Dr. Joni: You will blow her mind by offering to help! You have to start thinking about banking those love points!

We know what you're probably thinking: Why are we talking about dry cleaning? I want to talk about sex! Well, that's the point. Men and women are *very* different. You have to start small because you need to get her to like you enough to even consider wanting to have sex with you, tonight or any other night. Women are emotional creatures. We have to be warmed up, priming the pump so to speak, and the best way to begin doing that is to show interest. Communication is the easiest way to begin to let her know that you are genuinely interested in her and how she is feeling. Just that little interaction exampled above, done our way, will earn you at least a kiss on the cheek and a weary satisfied smile. This is a first step toward her wanting you, and more often!

This may seem like a trivial example of everyday life, but a deep, sexually rich relationship is made up of thousands of moments just like this. We know you find that hard to believe because men think differently. It is easy for men to compartmentalize. You can be pissed off that your wife may have forgotten to pick up your shirts, but if she feels randy a couple of hours later, your attitude is "what shirts?" right? For her, it is more difficult to let go of her aggravation to get to a place where she feels aroused.

Always remember that you catch more flies with honey than vinegar. (There's a reason some sayings are clichés—they're true!)

OK, so you have earned a few bonus points by offering to pick up your dry cleaning. What's next? There are an infinite number of little ways that you can better your chances of putting your partner in the mood that have nothing to do with sex. You need to get a little creative and stay present. We know it feels like you're taking the long route to your own bedroom, but be patient. It will pay off, we promise! You'll be amazed at how much better your sex life will be after you try our suggestions, so hang on!

Think of it this way: you need to build up an account, filled with good deeds, romantic hints, and generally sweet behavior, in order to increase your partner's desire to want you sexually. Like a savings account, your romance account is built by making regular deposits. **The size of the deposit is not as important as the frequency**. When you are more loving and attentive, your partner will notice that you have sincerely changed for the better. The more consistent you are, the closer she is going to feel to you. When your woman feels like you are there for her, lightening her load, being supportive, and increasing the frequency of compliments and other romantic gestures, she will begin to fall in love with you all over again...through new eyes. (There's a biological reason for this too: women need to feel bonded to you to want to make love. It's how her different brain chemicals combine with her estrogen, letting her know that you were the best choice as a mate.) So what happens when we all first fall in love? We want to make love all the time. Focus on the little things first, and then worry about getting physical. Here are a few examples of ways to increase the balance in your romance bank account:

🦋 Offer to do household chores without being asked.

Examples include vacuuming, taking out the trash, doing the dishes or loading the dishwasher, emptying the dryer and folding the clothes, changing the sheets on the bed, etc. There are thousands of little things that she does every week, things that just get magically done without you lifting a finger. Offering to help is as important as actually helping. The fact that you notice that there is a lot to do to keep your lives running smoothly is a big deal to her, and she will appreciate it more than you can fathom. And when you help, the added bonus is that you also get to spend more time together.

Dr. Joni: And that gives you both more time and energy for intimacy!

Esther: Find the chores you don't mind doing together, and get ready to turn it into a fiery sexcapade, because later we'll show you how to incorporate a little sexy fantasy into everyday life!

🦋 Offer to do parenting chores without being asked.

Not only will your spouse be thrilled, but your kids will be too. And nothing warms a woman's heart like seeing her man bond with his children. Examples are things like offering to bathe the kids, going outside and playing catch or tag, reading them a bedtime story, or being the parent to comfort your child when a bad dream strikes in the middle of the night.

Warning: We do not recommend doing any activities with the kids that will raise the noise level in the house. Many women tend to get more noise sensitive as the day wears on, especially when they are premenstrual. (We'll bet you didn't know that.) Besides, you don't want to wind the kids up; you want to calm them down, so that the grown-ups can have some quiet and personal time. (If the kids need to burn off some energy, take them outdoors to do it.)

Compliments go a long way, especially when they are unsolicited.
When she gets dressed, tell her she looks beautiful...and mean it. Tell her if the color she's wearing brings out the colors in her eyes. (Yes, most eyes have several colors in them. Take a closer look.) If you notice gold flecks in her eyes then mention them. Do her eyes change color based on her mood? Try to notice what color they are when she is laughing or happy. If she puts something on that makes her look slender, then **say** so. Don't wait for her to ask you if it makes her look fat. And don't **ever** tell her she looks fat. That will result in a sharp decline in your romance account.

Women are typically insecure about their appearance unless they are in perfect shape (and even then they have their moments), so you cannot tell her often enough how great she looks, feels, smells, tastes...you get the idea. Women are semantic by nature. We revel in words and their endless meanings, so expand your vocabulary: great, sexy, beautiful, delicious, edible, delectable, good enough to eat.... Have fun with it. She will! She needs to hear the words often!

Compliments: Your New Vocabulary

For those of you who are not very creative, here is a short cheat sheet with the right words to flatter your woman, her cooking, her lovemaking…you get the idea…

- Beautiful
- Delicious
- Good Enough to Eat
- Sexy
- Amazing
- Excellent
- Marvelous
- Really Hot
- I want you now!
- You look so hot, I wish we had time to….
- This tastes almost as good as you do
- Let's start with dessert…
- No woman has every looked as pretty as you do
- You take my breath away

Use the words "I love you" as often as possible. For women, these are the three most beautiful words in any language. The underlying problem here is that you need to communicate your love message in a way that she will hear it. That means small gifts are a good idea, or physical affection, and of course compliments that tell why you love her. Those are always a big hit. We know that for you, making love is a great way to say "I love you," but that won't work for her. And forget about unsolicited advice; it's not a woman's idea of an expression of love…sorry! Many women will subconsciously take this as criticism, which is way too much like a father figure, not a loving partner and friend.

🌶 Show your woman that you appreciate her and the way she loves you.

This is not about gift giving; it's about communicating your appreciation in a way that she will hear it, in her language. Dr. Karen Gail Lewis, in her book *Why Don't You Understand? A Gender Relationship Dictionary*, has a great analogy for how men and women look at relationships differently. She calls it the "Shoebox/Mantel" dichotomy. Men take something they treasure, like a prized baseball card, a genuine arrowhead found in childhood, or their relationship, and put it in a safe place where they can treasure it and go look at it whenever they need to, but they know it is safe and secure. Women are the opposite. We take a prized possession (a piece of artwork, a special photograph) and display it for the world to see because, when it's visible, it can be appreciated. We do the same thing with relationships. We want everyone to notice and admire this amazing love we have.

Do something that will speak to her "mantel" mentality: a mushy card, flowers, something that reminds you of her, or a piece of jewelry works wonders. (That's why women love jewelry—we get to show it off and it says "Look how much he loves me!")

Dr. Joni: Want something fun? Try a musical card. I was having a really bad day and Esther gave me a musical card that warmed my heart and made me feel so special and I could not stop smiling for the rest of the day.

🌸 Bring her flowers—for no reason at all.

Many of you reading this live in a city where street vendors abound, with easy-to-grab bouquets at great prices. Does she have a favorite flower? Do you even know what it is? Find out by watching movies together and keep your eyes open for flowers in the background, and ask her if she likes the ones you see. What kind of flowers did you have at your wedding and in her bouquet? Check the pictures. If you don't recognize them, take the picture to your local florist for help.

Suggestion: Unless you know she loves them, do not bring her carnations; they're perceived by women as cheap and used for funerals. Beware of lilies too; they are also a popular funeral flower, and their pungent odor can make many turn up their noses.

Esther: If money is tight, try a single red rose. It's not about the amount of money you spend or the size of the bouquet, it's the effort and the sentiment behind it that matters most.

Tip: Can't afford flowers? Try a card instead. Look for one that says the things that you have trouble expressing. This is great for you strong, silent types.

Sometimes a woman just needs a little reminder of how you feel.

Offer to cook dinner.

If the prospect of cooking terrifies you, then offer to help. Nothing turns a woman on more than someone else cooking her dinner...and cleaning up. If the kitchen is too intimidating for you, then offer to clean up. It's the least you can do. If you would like to deal with your fear of food preparation, start watching the cooking channels. It's actually fun, and you can find a lot of great ideas for awesome dishes that are easy to prepare. Around Valentine's Day, the food networks feature amazing romantic meals and desserts that range in levels of difficulty to create. Give it a try; she will flip! Still terrified? How about "take in"? I bet some of her favorite restaurants will let you pick up dinners, and some may even deliver. Set the food on your own dishes, and you have a hot romantic meal at your fingertips. For some easy, sexy meals, check out the chapter on using food for seduction.

Dr. Joni: Add flowers and candles for bonus points!

Bring home a nice bottle of wine for no reason (if she drinks).

Pour her a glass and plant a little kiss on her cheek or lips (if she offers them) and tell her you're going to take the kids outside to shoot hoops, or play so that she can have a few moments of peace, or the time to cook dinner in peace. If there are no children in the background, or if they are old enough to be quietly attending to their homework, pour yourself a glass too, and when she asks you what the special occasion is, tell her coming home to her is reason enough to celebrate. Maybe you're just getting wiser with age... you are realizing that life is about celebrating the little moments together, as well as the big accomplishments and special occasions.

Esther: Nothing signifies a celebration like champagne. Talk about romantic!

Dr. Joni: If she doesn't drink, how about making her a steaming cup of her favorite tea or hot chocolate? If you're not sure what she prefers, ask!

🖋 Create a peace accord for downtime upon arriving home after work.

Many men need a half hour to decompress after work. If you work a physical job, you may want to come home, drop your dirty clothes and get cleaned up before relaxing in your favorite chair. Have a conversation with your partner that you will be happy to help her around the house after you have had an opportunity to chill out. Let her know what chores you are willing to do and that you are comfortable with giving her the same chance to let go of her day so you can then sit down together in a more relaxed state of mind. Your chill out time can be together or solo, whatever works best for both of you.

Why Don't Relationships Come with Subtitles?
A List of Things To NEVER Do

Okay, boys, this book is for you, so let's try to shed a little light on a not so well kept secret: women and men speak different languages. Do you ever feel like she just doesn't understand the words coming out of your mouth? Well, you're not crazy. Men and women have very different speech patterns and a totally different approach to language, the definitions, and the uses of words. It would take a whole book to discuss the differences in language usage between the sexes, and there are a few great ones out there. One of our favorites is <u>Every Man Sees You Naked</u> by David Matthews. It's a hysterical read that lets women know how to effectively communicate with their men based on how men think. We are also grateful to Dr. Karen Gail Lewis for her work <u>Why Don't You Understand? A Gender Relationship Dictionary</u>, which also sheds light onto the verbal battle of the sexes and how to avoid bloodshed. Here's our list of things to **NEVER** do that might help you avoid the next round before the bell rings:

Never offer unsolicited advice.

We understand that, for most men, advice is an expression of love, helping to solve a problem. That's what you boys do best—you are problem solvers by nature. The only problem with this line of thinking is this: when your woman is telling you about a situation she is faced with, she may not want a solution from you; she may just want you to give her the opportunity to vent and for you to listen and care. Your best bet: When she is verbally spent, ask her if she would like a suggestion before offering your sage advice. This way, she gets to decide if she wants a solution or if all she needed was the opportunity to vent; that way, she could discover that she knew the answer to her problem all along. Of course, if she asks for your input, then you have a green light to lend a helping hand.

Never Use Overtly General Words like "Fine", "Nice", & "Okay".

You must eliminate words that are trite and not specific. We have great faith in you that you can come up with something sexier to say than that! Avoid words that can be construed as having negative overtones, like curvy (unless you clearly mean it as a compliment), zaftig, fat, unflattering, a little tight, etc. Weight is a dangerous topic for all women, so if you don't like how something looks on her, get up, go into her closet, and find something that you like on her...something she has worn in the past six months please, and ask her to try that on instead so you can compare it. Tell her you like your choice because she looked sexy in it the last time you saw it on her, and she'll put it on immediately. If you're shopping together (you brave soul, you) watch what sizes she is picking up. If you don't like something, go looking in the similar size or one size larger and just bring her something you would like her to try on, and be sure it's something sexy and revealing. Even if she doesn't buy it, this action will let her know you find her sexy no matter what size she is, and you get to see her in something sexy and revealing—bonus!

Here's the biggest difference in our uses of language: men are literal, and women look for the layers in the words you say. When you use phrases like "either dress is fine" or "you can pick where we go for dinner", she interprets that as you don't care rather than either dress is fine or you don't care what kind of food they serve, as long as you get fed. So be specific and clear. If she looks at you like "I can't believe you said that", just tell her "I prefer you with nothing on at all, but since you can't go to dinner naked, both dresses make you look good enough to eat, so you pick which one is more comfortable" or "I have great faith in you, and I can't make one more decision today, so you get to pick what we eat for dinner". Or, "I may just have to eat you, which can be arranged. Should I save that idea for dessert?"

Touch: The Next Frontier

So let's say that for the past week you've been a more supportive partner, a better dad, and you've brought home flowers. Now you can begin to involve physical contact. (This applies if you already have a good relationship. If you've been bickering or distant until reading this book, you may have to give these initial changes at least a couple of weeks to work, before trying to break the touch barrier. Consistent behavior will also ensure that she understands that these changes are more than temporary.) **There is a big difference between sexual touch and romantic touch.**

We know that it can be subtle, but for women, there is a definite difference. Romantic touch is about making a physical and emotional connection and, in many cases, repairing bridges that have broken down due to neglect. Romantic touch may lead to something more, even sexual touch, but sometimes a kiss is just a kiss. At first we want you to just focus on making the initial physical connection. You are making these changes for life. Time is on your side. What you must always remember is that like sweet deeds, increasing the frequency of romantic forms of touch adds points to your Romance Account. It is the frequency, and in this case, the fact that you are satisfied that a touch doesn't have to lead to something sexual, that will build not only trust with your partner, it will also build credibility for your actions.

Many women will read into occasional romantic caresses, thinking all that you really want is sex. If you show her that you want more than just a sexual encounter, that your goal is a sexier, more passionate relationship as a whole, her response will be less suspicious, and her surprise will lead to satisfaction. By raising the touch factor of your relationship to a higher level, you are not only improving your level of communication, you are also making each other feel sexier on a daily basis. When women feel sexy and begin to perceive their relationship as a passionate existence, it leads to wanting sexual experiences with our partner more often. Once you master this level of romantic touch, both of you will be ready to naturally progress to the next level, and become more intimate.

These are the first recommendations for touch, so please **make sure that you precede it with being more attentive and involved, using the suggestions above, or she's going to think you want something, probably sex**. That's not the way to get her in the mood; it will probably just irritate her.

Remember, this is about bonding and reestablishing your romantic relationship, not about sex...yet. Try these suggestions for creating a new level of physical intimacy:

When you're watching television, sit next to her. Always ask permission before touching her. You might try "May I hold your hand?" This will let her know you want to touch her, and that kind of communication will build trust. Reach for her hand and just hold it. If you want, you may massage her hands. Or put your arm around her, so she can snuggle in your arms. Let her pick what to watch, especially if there are no kids present. If it's a "chick flick," watch it with her and watch what moves her. You are learning what turns her on, from everything around her including colors, music, flowers, and seduction scenes in a movie. Remember, this is about intimacy and closeness right now, not sex. If she feels closer to you, she will be more inclined to think about having sex. The more information you have about what turns her on, the more ammunition you have in your love arsenal.

Esther: If you're dying to watch something she has no interest in, like a game or wrestling, offer to give her something in return. One couple we know has this deal: he gets to watch wrestling if she can put her head in his lap and he massages her head, and runs his fingers through her hair. She gets the physical affection she craves, and he gets to watch what he wants; it's a win-win for everybody!

🦋 **When she's cooking dinner, walk up behind her (not while she's wielding a knife, please), slip your arms around her waist, and plant a soft kiss on the back of her neck.**
You can also try just planting the kiss on her neck if the hug is too much right now; your goal is to break the touch barrier. Any attempt to reach out to her physically will be noticed and appreciated.

Dr. Joni: Try rubbing her shoulders and thanking her for preparing dinner. She'll be amazed and think you've been a victim of an attack by body snatchers, but she'll love it!

Has It Been a Really Long Time Since You & Your Partner Were Intimate?

Standing At The Crossroads

Life happens. Babies are born. Illnesses invade our lives. And stressful times at work can wreak havoc on our libidos. We understand that all relationships go through "dry spells". But, what if a dry spell has turned into the status quo? What happens when it's been a really long time since you've made love, and you're unsure of how to get back on the path to find each other again?

What's a long time? Well, 3 months is going to be our line in the sand. In the case of childbirth, after 90 days, your bundle of joy is starting to sleep a little more regularly, post partum depression should be lifting (if not, seek medical attention), and any surgical ramifications of a difficult childbirth should be healing nicely. In cases of prolonged illness, it is our contention that it takes both partners to decide that nothing is going to stand in the way of your commitment to each other to be Love Warriors—living without passion is not an option. (Please see our chapter Maintaining Intimacy During Times Of Illness & Bumps In The Road.)

When illness or childbirth is not the reason why intimacy has waned, then your challenge is to address what the problem really is. Has your relationship become a victim of neglect? Has one or both of you strayed from the relationship? Is the core of your problem a lack of communication? How do you build a bridge back to one another and recommit to the love that brought you together in the first place?

One of our favorite books on this topic is Dr. Beth Erickson's **Marriage isn't for Sissies: 7 Simple Keys to Unlocking The Best Part of Your Life**. Start today! Decide together that you want this, that your relationship is worth saving, and commit to doing the work that it takes to build that bridge, one step at a time. Dr. Beth's book is a simple way to apply a set of steps that make reconnecting fun and easy. It's also a great book to read together, in bed. Our favorite Key: The Daily Magic Ten Minutes. Commit to spending ten minutes each day together—alone. That means no kids, no dogs, no phones or email, and no television. And you can't talk about work, the kids, or any other source of stress. You get to talk about cool things that bring you closer and give you a glimpse into the inner world of your beloved. Want to take a fantasy vacation to an exotic destination? Want to discuss a hobby you've always wanted to try or a sport you've wanted to master or a language you want to learn? How about discussing things you might want to do together, like taking samba lessons or a cooking class? Take a 10 minute journey – with your passionate future being your destination. Reconnecting on this level will bring you closer, and, soon, you may find that you are holding hands when you walk the dog, or pouring a glass of wine for your ten minutes, and playing footsie on the balcony. Can passion be very far behind?

The point of this whole conversation is that you must be committed to strengthening your relationship as a whole. You see, women want to feel loved. When they feel loved, it leads them to feeling sexy. When women feel sexy and loved, they feel like having sex. We can't stress this enough. Women are emotional creatures, so we need to be stimulated emotionally. Once we are emotionally stimulated, it is a natural progression to having the desire for sex. It will be more difficult to encourage her to have sex more often if she doesn't feel emotionally close to you right now. Your first task is to get her to like you again. You do that by becoming a new man: more attentive, more caring, and more helpful. You're more thoughtful too, bringing home flowers for no reason, picking up a half gallon of milk on your way home because you noticed this morning over coffee that you were almost out, and taking a turn bathing the kids or chasing them around outside to burn off some energy while she cooks dinner or just sits peacefully sipping a glass of wine.

Esther: You will be amazed at how different your life will become once you start introducing this level of touch into every day. Here's

---

an idea—how about dancing together? Waiting for dinner to be ready? Twirl her around a little before sundown and see what happens once the kids are asleep!

There is an important reason we are spending so much time on communication. When you do get reconnected, and you will, there will be a time when you will need to communicate about intimate details of your lovemaking— what feels good and what doesn't. To be able to have that level of comfort with each other, you have to start somewhere, and talking about the everyday details of life in a caring and observant way will lead to deeper discussions, where you will both be comfortable enough to open up and be honest concerning topics you may have neglected to mention for a long time. This may seem elementary, but have faith; your patience will be rewarded soon enough.

Your next task is to reconnect on a physical level using romantic touch. Soft kisses, holding hands in front of the television, snuggling while watching a movie, and scratching her back are all easy ways to bridge the gap if there hasn't been a lot of touching lately. The more often you reach out to her physically, the more consistent the changes in your behavior will seem. By reconnecting on both a verbal and physical level, you are reaffirming your commitment to your relationship and to your desire to grow that relationship on a core level. Once you have rebuilt these bridges, you are on your way to crossing them and recreating your sex life.

CHAPTER 3.
Two Languages of Love:
What Dialect Do You Speak?

Esther: During our research, we sifted through scores of books written by marriage and family counselors. Many had some valuable information about communication and how to avoid pitfalls down the road as your relationship tackles the many challenges life presents, but some of them stand out. One such book is *Your Ex Factor* by Dr. Stephan Poulter. His insightful and articulate work has shed a bright light on the nature of love and how to deepen not only your love for each other but also how to expand your own capacity for being loved. We highly recommend it for your relationship survival library. This chapter is inspired by Stephan's work, and we are grateful to him for the inspiration to love he has provided.

Our culture fails to teach us how to look deep within ourselves and figure out who we are and what we want. When it comes to love, things are no different. While you might get lucky and find a partner who is a master communicator and can tell you exactly what she wants you to do to her and for her in order for her to feel adored and cherished, the sad reality is that most of us are groping around in the dark, literally and figuratively, for what works best to make each other happy. In his book, *Your Ex Factor—Overcome Heartbreak and Build a Better Life*, Dr. Stephan Poulter says it best: we have to first understand ourselves and how we like to be loved before we can ever hope to understand someone else.

OK, great idea. How do we do that? First, it's time to figure out your personal love style. Dr. Poulter identifies five primary styles of feeling loved: verbal, physical/sexual contact, gestures/actions, companionship, and acceptance. What do these mean? These are the ways each of us needs to be communicated with in order to feel loved. In other words, do you like to hear the words "I love you" from your partner and have deep meaningful conversations to warm your heart, or do you want/need sex or physical contact to feel loved? Some people prefer gestures, like doing things for them (filling up the gas tank in their car, paying for house repairs, doing chores without being asked) as signs of love and devotion. Some people prefer to spend time together to feel that connection. How you like to feel loved is your own unique love language.

Here's the challenge in every relationship: once you have identified what you need to feel loved, how do you communicate that to your partner? Do you know what she needs to feel loved? This is one of the biggest minefields of all relationships—the assumption that your partner will innately know how to love you and give you exactly what you need to feel loved, cherished, and adored. This assumption can lead to communication breakdowns, heartache, and eventually the dissolution of your relationship if you let it. **Understanding how you and your partner need to be loved and sharing that information clearly and lovingly is a guaranteed way to revitalize and transform your relationship no matter where you are today.**

What makes us feel loved?

Love is about action. How you feel loved is about communicating your love language to each other, giving you both the opportunity to transform that information into daily behaviors that resonate with your hearts. There are five forms of action that make us feel loved:

- Affection
- Communication
- Intimacy
- Compatibility
- Stress/conflict resolution

The clearer you are with each other about what specific actions in each category you like and dislike, the easier it will be for you to make each other happy. One of the many reasons we love Dr. Poulter's book is that he is clear that it is your first and foremost responsibility to figure out how **you** like to be loved, and then to communicate that lovingly to your partner. We all speak a specific love language, and you can't expect to have successful communication with someone if you are speaking Chinese and they are speaking Greek. This language of intimacy is individual, like your fingerprint. What works for you may not work for anyone else, but it is right for you, and it's necessary for your happiness. The best part about love is that, at our core, we want to make the person we love happy, whatever that means for him or her. So, you may have to stretch out of your comfort zone to find out what you need and what she needs to feel loved and cherished. Once you start communicating in her love language and she communicates in yours, you will watch in amazement how much deeper and richer your connection to each other becomes.

"Love can be understood only 'from the
inside,' as a language can be
understood only by someone who speaks it, as a world
can be understood only by someone who lives in it."
–Robert C. Solomon, philosopher

Let's Get Specific: A Couple's Exercise

Esther: This exercise is adapted from *Your Ex-Factor: Overcome Heartbreak and Build a Better Life,* by Stephen B. Poulter (Amherst, NY: Prometheus Books, 2009), pp. 232-235. Copyright (c) 2009 by Stephen B. Poulter. Used with permission of Prometheus Books, www.prometheusbooks.com.

The bottom line is this: the better you are at communicating what you each need to feel loved, the better shot you each stand of getting it. OK, boys, you are going to need to have a chat. Yes, talking about love is a requirement, but it doesn't have to be painful! Here is an easy quiz to get the conversation started, and let's make this fun. This is about connecting with your woman and finding out what she needs to feel loved. You want to be her hero, right? This will also give her some insight into what makes you tick and what makes you feel all warm and tingly inside. The level of connection this exercise will give you will catapult you to a new level of communication. It's a short walk from communicating better to having great sex! Let's get started.

Two Languages of Love: What Dialect Do You Speak?

Instructions: Make a copy of these questions for each of you and answer them privately and honestly. When you are both done, sit down together—in front of a fire, on the beach, in the backyard, with your favorite beverage, an open mind, and an open heart—and discuss your answers in a gentle, loving manner. Be sure to listen. If you are not clear about anything she says, stop and ask for more information. This is a fact-finding mission. Treat it with the military precision of a full-scale espionage assignment, and you will be rewarded!

Affection
1. Do you enjoy holding hands, hugging, touching, and giving/getting back rubs?
2. Is eye contact important?
3. Do you like public displays of affection, or is physical affection something you enjoy only in private?
4. Do you enjoy touching base with your partner during your day apart—phone calls, e-mails, text messages—expressing that she is thinking of you?
5. Do you enjoy unexpected gifts?
6. Do you like to cuddle and be physically close?
7. Do you like to be touched (nonsexually)?
8. Do you enjoy it when your partner makes you a drink, or reaches out after a misunderstanding, or takes the kids outside to burn off some energy and give you a break?

Communication
1. Do enjoy discussing all aspects of your life—work, home life, goals, dreams—with your partner?
2. Is there anything you are not comfortable sharing with your partner?
3. How do you communicate when you are angry or upset—screaming, silent treatment, avoidance?

4. Are you comfortable discussing and asking your partner for what you need physically, emotionally, and sexually? Are you comfortable asking for physical and emotional affection?
5. Is it important to you to discuss your feelings when you are angry, depressed, or excited?
6. When you are upset, how do you like your partner to communicate with you? Listen only, offer advice, be supportive?
7. Has communication over hot topics been difficult in the past for you as a couple?

Intimacy

1. What activities, gestures and topics of discussion make you feel emotionally connected to your partner?
2. How often do you like to have sex?
3. Do you enjoy physical intimacy that is sexually charged, like foreplay, kissing, hand-holding, foot rubs, hugs, oral sex?
4. Do you like to be pursued sexually or do you like to do the pursuing?
5. Is it important to you to spend free time together?
6. Do you like doing couple activities together?
7. Does your partner know from direct communication from you what you want and need when it comes to intimacy and sexual gratification?
8. Do you expect your partner to understand your wishes because of the information you have shared?

Compatibility

1. How important is your partner's physical appearance to you?
2. Is a physically active lifestyle important to you? Would you like to incorporate more physical activity into

your relationship as a way to spend time together and live a healthier lifestyle?

3. Are your spiritual beliefs important in your relationship?
4. What are your feelings around money? Are you comfortable discussing issues of finance—saving, spending, investments—with your partner?
5. How important is sexual appetite to you? Would you be willing to do whatever it takes to stay connected even if your appetites are not on the same level?
6. How much attention do you need to feel loved?
7. Do you see yourself as a social person or a wall flower? Are your personality styles different? Are they complimentary?
8. How do you prefer to have your partner express their feelings: verbally, sexually, emotionally, or in writing?

Stress/Conflict Resolution
1. What do you need from your partner when you are stressed out or upset?
2. When you have small disagreements, do you hold a grudge or are you easy to forgive small transgressions?
3. Do you like to work out conflicts or do you avoid them like the plague?
4. Do you yell, argue, defend, name-call, or get physical when you get angry?
5. Do your partner's strong expressions of anger frighten you?
6. Are you open and honest about things you are ashamed of or secretive about with your partner?
7. What is the one thing you won't tolerate when arguing?
8. What is the perfect conflict resolution scenario for you?

Love Her Right

Now that you are really in touch with what each of you wants and needs to feel loved, it's time to clue you in on a few more secrets about what makes your beautiful woman tick. This is all new information for most of you, so get excited because the more you understand about women, the easier it will be to stay connected with your woman! And the things we know are a little sexy....

Part Two: Applying What You Have Learned So Far

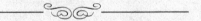

"Those people who develop the ability to continuously acquire new and better forms of knowledge that they can apply to their work and to their lives will be the movers and shakers in our society for the indefinite future."
—Brian Tracy author & sales trainer

CHAPTER 4.
Couple Time:
Making Romance A Priority

In a previous chapter, we taught you about the language of love. Hopefully, you and your partner have taken the quiz at the end of that chapter and shared your results. It's important that you try it because the more information you have about what each of you needs to feel loved, cherished, and adored, the easier this section is going to be to execute. Now it is time to take that translation dictionary you have created, filled with her definitions of love, and apply them to real-life action. It's time to begin looking at your life and finding ways to make it a sexier existence for both of you.

Let's face it, we live in a crazy, hectic world. Life is so busy that we forget to make time for the important things, like spending quality time together. Romance is becoming a lost art, and it is high time we breathe life back into this most vital part of our human experience. How do we do it?

Begin to Spend Quality Time Together

With all of the things on your schedule, you might be forgetting to make time to spend solely with the one you love. That means no kids, no in-laws, and no distractions—just you and your woman. Remember when you first were getting to know each other? What did you do? You went on dates. Just because you're married, or committed to each other, and possibly have children in the picture, doesn't mean you can't go on romantic dates now. Dedicating specific times to be together romantically is important. It means that you are making your relationship a priority and that romance is important to you. Simply making that statement, through your actions as well as your words, will increase your Romance Account by leaps and bounds. Your partner needs to know, and see, that creating romance in your relationship is important to you, and when she does, it makes her love you and want you more.

> **Get your kids on board with the concept of "Mommy and Daddy time."**
> For those of you with children, we have to start here. Your children will learn about love, romance, and marriage from you. Teach them by example that love, and maintaining love and romance, is a lifelong adventure. Much like parenting, keeping romance alive takes daily vigilance and an undercurrent of dedication to your relationship. Recruit your kids into your mission of creating alone time for the two of you, and reward them for understanding that you and your partner need this time together. If you plan a weekend away with your spouse, get the kids to help you plan the next retreat that will include them—a day at an action park, a camping trip, or even pizza and the opening of a new kids' movie will make them cheer and absolve you of any parental guilt you have in planning and executing an excursion without them. This also means that you are actively planning quality time with your kids, something all of you will appreciate today and tomorrow.

DR. JONI and ESTHER: WHILE THINKING ABOUT THIS, IT DAWNED ON US THAT THOSE OF YOU WITH KIDS MAY BE RESISTANT TO HAVING STRANGERS WATCH YOUR CHILDREN, AND MAY BE WITHOUT FAMILY CLOSE BY TO HELP WITH YOUR ACHIEVING COUPLE TIME. WE CAME UP WITH A BRILLIANT IDEA—HOW ABOUT CREATING A COUPLE TIME SUPPORT TEAM WITH YOUR FRIENDS THAT ARE ALSO PARENTS? PLAN A GET-TOGETHER AND DISCUSS THE POSSIBILITY OF TAKING TURNS WATCHING EACH OTHER'S KIDS. THIS WILL GIVE EACH COUPLE THE OPPORTUNITY TO ENHANCE THEIR RELATIONSHIP BY SPENDING QUALITY TIME TOGETHER WITHOUT CHILDREN. MAKE SURE YOU ALL GET EQUAL COUPLE TIME, AND THAT THE KIDS GET ALONG BEFORE CHOOSING PLAYDATES. IF YOUR ADULT FRIENDS DON'T HAVE KIDS OR THE AGE DIFFERENCES DON'T WORK, WHAT ABOUT YOUR KIDS' FRIENDS? DO YOU KNOW THEIR PARENTS WELL ENOUGH TO BRING UP THE TOPIC—THEY MIGHT BE MORE INTERESTED THAN YOU KNOW!

🌢 **Here is a great way to connect on a daily basis. Incorporate an exercise called The Daily Magic Ten Minutes.** As we mentioned earlier, this is a great suggestion from our friend Dr. Beth Erickson and her awesome book *Marriage Isn't For Sissies*, and this exercise is easy and fun! Just commit to spending ten minutes together as a couple every day, but there's a catch! You can talk about anything **except** the kids, work, money (any source of stress in your relationship), and no distractions—no kids, dogs, cell phones, or in-laws. Just the two of you and a glass of wine or a cup of coffee and a chat about your next adventure, or a hobby you're interested in.

Think of it as a daily opportunity to rediscover your lover and fall for her all over again!

🐾 **Incorporate fun and healthy activities that get you moving and get you connected.** Try an evening walk. Take the dog and you can even take the kids if they're too young to leave alone. A walk never killed anyone, and it sure beats another thirty minutes of a rerun you've seen anyway. (Don't worry; the television will still be there when you get back!) Fresh air, a change of scenery, and the opportunity for the kids and animals to burn off a little of their frenetic energy before bedtime will help everyone sleep better. Do you have a park, a forest, or a beach nearby? Try mixing up your excursions and take in the beauty of the world we live in, even if it's your own backyard. Pick her a flower, chase the kids, act silly, hold her hand, remind her of the crazy guy she fell in love with a lifetime ago, and you will touch her heart, which is only a short distance from stoking her fires!

🐾 **Try something you have never done before together.** Have you ever wanted to jump out of an airplane, take a hot air balloon ride, horseback ride, spend a day at the batting cages or a shooting range, or take a hot yoga or cooking class? This is a fun thing to use as conversation for the Daily Magic Ten Minutes, so try it out. Make sure that you give each other equal time; pick things to try that each of you wants to do and take turns. Remember, this is about getting closer as a couple, so you may have to stretch out of your comfort zone a bit. If she wants to take a cooking class or try hot yoga, don't give her grief over it; just try it. You may not love everything you try, but the effort you put forth, with love and a sense of humor, will make her fall in love with you all over again! Besides, yoga will make you both more flexible for sex play, and cooking lessons will help you immeasurably for your next mission: seduction!

Dr. Joni: If finances are tight and child care is an issue, how about trying an instructional DVD? You can learn a new language, visit exotic locales while learning the history, try a new workout or learn how to cook. The kids will enjoy this too!

🖉 **Create a project to work on together.** Have you ever wanted to build a birdhouse, write a book, learn a language, or start a home business? Do it, and make it a project that you work on together, as a way to bring you closer. We are lucky. We love to spend the majority of our time together, so we began the Love Her Right project to be able to one day do just that. Today, we work from home together and spend the whole day together working on writing, radio show production, Web site maintenance, doing interviews, and a host of other things. What began as a project of love turned into a lifestyle that works for our relationship. If you love spending time together and want to create an opportunity to separate your lives from the rat race, find something that you both want to create, do, be, or sell, and make it happen. The only thing you will sacrifice is television time. What you will gain will transform your relationship and can transform your bank account and your life.

The commitment to spend more time together is necessary for both of you to make, so don't expect her to plan all the romantic encounters—planning them is half the fun. This can be accomplished without having a lot of extra money. A romantic interlude can be as simple as cooking her a nice dinner, bringing in take out, or picking out a romantic movie to watch while cuddled up on the couch. Of course, going out is also romantic, and with the help of a little extra cash, you could even spring for a night or a weekend at a romantic hotel. The possibilities are endless and only limited by your imagination.

- **Vacation Sex is the best.** There are no distractions, no other obligations, just the two of you, all romance, all the time. If you can get away, just the two of you, even if it's only for a weekend, do it. Save up for it, and make this kind of romantic quality time a priority. It will bring you closer as a couple and give you the opportunity to focus solely on each other...and what turns you on!

Esther: If you have been bitten by the travel bug like us, make some of your trips true adventures. Joni makes it her mission to research any new place we decide to go. She learns the local customs, researches the best sights to see and places to eat (we love food), and even learns a little of the language. Me, I love to plan the vacations where we do nothing—a great beach, tropical waters, a drink with a little umbrella, and guilty pleasures like rich food and afternoon sex! We take turns making the plans and deciding what kind of vacation we need—a chill out, relax, and rejuvenate trip or a discovery mission to inspire and delight the senses. Did you know that almost 80 percent of Americans don't use all their vacation time every year? You owe it to yourself—for your health and for the health of your relationship—to take your vacation time and nurture your body and spirit. On one's deathbed, no one will say, "I wish I spent more time at work." Make living life your priority, and watch what happens to your world. It will be like landing in Oz, when all of your surroundings go from black and white to Technicolor. Don't take our word for it—try it and find out!

Dr. Joni: If finances are tough, try starting with an "I Love You" account. That means every time that one of you says "I love you" the other person has to put $.25 in a jar. The more you can afford, the sooner you will have funds for a trip or excursion! If expenses really don't allow any other alternatives, try taking a vacation day or two at home, and transform your home into a vacation destination. Play the right music, rent a movie that is set in an exotic locale, and take in or prepare a meal similar to what you would have on this fantasy trip. Imagination is a great tool, and you can incorporate the kids on this fantasy trip too!

Spending time together can be fun, exciting, and filled with new experiences. Start today! You can even begin by asking your spouse to read this chapter, and ask her what she thinks! Women love romance, and romance to women has many meanings—not just flowers, chocolates, and candlelight. Spending time with your children, doing things together that she wants to try that may not be your idea of a good time, or just enjoying a chat about a fantasy vacation over a quiet glass of wine at sunset will put a twinkle in her eye and warmth in her heart. Now it's time to take that warmth and spread it south of the border. How? It's time to talk about the next step and start to get sexy: seduction! Next, we're going to talk about getting sexy with food. Did you know that certain foods can put you "in the mood"? So come on, Romeo, let's learn how you can cook in the kitchen and the bedroom!

CHAPTER 5.
Get Cooking With Foods That Make You Feel Sexy!

So, we're going to talk about your tongue a lot, especially it's usage for kissing and oral sex. But did you know that the human tongue has 10,000 taste buds? Some of them are located on the roof of the mouth as well. You have different kinds of taste buds: sweet, salt, bitter, and more. Did you know that taste is affected by your ability or inability to smell? Taste and smell work together, which is why, when you have a cold, you can't taste as well as normal. So why do you care? Certain tastes and smells in certain foods are actually aphrodisiacs—things that turn us on! So why not add simple scents and flavors to your bag of tricks to fire up your love life and your meals? Let's plan a seduction over a meal. People connect over food, and sexy foods start to set the scene!

Dr. Joni loves to cook and is an amazing chef, and even learned from Julia Child. She has also studied aromatherapy, which incorporates scents that turn on certain parts of your brain. Since we believe that food is life and sex is a part of life, why not combine the two for an exciting experience while dining? OK, so not everyone is a gourmet chef, but you don't have to be. Just cooking for your partner and taking the responsibility from her shoulders is something that she will totally appreciate. Showing her that you love her in this way is a turn-on just because you tried! Combining flavors, textures, scents, and presentation can be easily picked up by anyone. It can even be accomplished with take-out food for the totally cooking phobic! So, let's start with some basics about what foods and spices work, why they work, and what part of you should get stimulated.

There will be differences in foods that you and your partner may or may not eat. Also, there may be concerns surrounding the calories associated with certain foods, especially when dealing with someone who has weight issues or food allergies. Whenever possible, we are going to try to give alternative lower-calorie choices to avoid messing with a commitment to eat healthier when all you wanted to do was to turn her on with a fun, sexy meal.

Dr. Joni: Make sure that you also have vibrant colors together on a plate to make it visually appealing, which is one of your senses that need arousal.

So, when picking out foods that are sexually stimulating, let's attach a few adjectives to give you some clues about what works. Think sensually: hot, fiery, sinful, luscious, steamy, gooey, and succulent! Combining sweet with spicy foods makes for a great mouthful of layers of flavors. Finger foods make for an intimate dining experience, especially when you feed your partner! Dripping, warm chocolate on a ripe berry can be eaten off her stomach for a fun romp! Don't forget to put a towel under her first to keep the cleanup easier!

OK, let's start with the food groups and which ones are the tops for nibbling and getting nibbled on.

FRUITS AND VEGETABLES

Acai Berries: The Brazilian Viagra!
Found in juice form, it is high in antioxidants and helps keep your heart and your blood flowing to the areas that

you want blood to flow to...especially your penis! Look for unfiltered juice; it also helps with arthritis, joint pain, and is vegan. The only complication is with diabetics...you need to eat protein before drinking the juice to balance out the sugar levels in your system. Acai has benefits for your heart, blood flow, and muscle health, and includes the micronutrients needed to keep you pumping! The huge dose of antioxidants also adds to your longevity, vitality, and virility. Live long, love hard, and stay hard! Our favorite version: Mona Vie, an amazing blend of eighteen high-antioxidant fruits from all over the world.

Artichokes:
The French swear by the aphrodisiac qualities of artichokes! Use a knife or scissors to cut off the spikes at the ends of the leaves first. Eat them steamed, or stuffed and then baked. You will know that they are cooked enough if you can easily stick a knife into the stem—about 15 – 20 minutes for steaming. Dip the leaves in a sauce or melted butter and scrape the meaty part from the leaves with your teeth... YUMMY! Scrape off the fuzzy part in the middle called the choke, discard that, and eat the base, known as the heart. Great for a finger food dinner! They can also be found in cans or jars, either marinated or in water if you can't be bothered and want to throw them into a dish with pasta along with garlic, olive oil, and if you have leftover chicken or another protein of choice. Heat them together, then sprinkle with a little grated parmesan or Romano cheese, chili pepper flakes, and voila...dinner!

Asparagus:
Very powerful, especially for men. It not only looks phallic, but is packed with potassium, phosphorus, calcium, and vitamin E. It gives you stamina, energy, and increased

hormone production. We recommend finding it fresh at your local market, as the ones in a can just do not do asparagus justice. They can be eaten cold after steaming or hot as a side dish.

Avocados:
When ripe, they are creamy, buttery, shaped like a woman, and melt on your tongue. Aztecs called them ahuacalt or testicle. Make guacamole a whole new experience!

Bananas:
Viagra-like effects and potassium too! Eat them fresh or sauté in butter and add a little maple syrup to put over ice cream for dessert. You can also cut them into chunks and dip them in chocolate too!

Beans:
Lima beans, string bean, baked beans, black beans—they all make you horny! Nuf said. Don't forget to take something like Beano if you are one who gets gassy.

Carrots:
Besides the vitamin A, they also look phallic and can be used in VERY creative ways. Eat them steamed, raw, or WHATEVER! Now you can see what or who you are eating.

Figs:
Talk about luscious, they are sweet, sexy, and put you in the mood. Raw, they are nature's delight, but difficult to find. Luckily, they can be found dried, and you can

simmer them in wine (ruby port works well) to plump them up and then serve with a soft, creamy cheese like goat cheese, or as a topping over ice cream. Or you can just feed them to each other and enjoy the fleshy sweetness. The tiny seeds are edible and add crunch to the sensation in your mouth.

Grapes:
When eaten raw, they are sweet and juicy. When they are fermented they make the nectar of the gods...wine and champagne. If you feel adventurous, take a soft cheese, cover the grape with the cheese, and roll them in chopped nuts. Feed them to your lover. Then, lick each other's fingers!

Mangos:
Sweet and tart, juicy and sensual, they supposedly help to strengthen the genitals. They are peeled, taken off the large pit in the middle, and are usually eaten raw. You can also use them as part of a fruit salsa for a topping on chicken or fish for a healthy and sexy summer dinner.

Mushrooms:
These are soft, wet, and juicy and can be filled with soft cheese or seafood. There are many varieties to try! Many of the Asian mushrooms, including shiitake and oyster, are believed to have healing properties as well. Try them sautéed, stuffed, or add to any meal.

Onions:
Greeks and ancient Hindus sing the praises of this stimulating vegetable. They are good for your heart too. You

should both eat them to not offend your partner with your breath. They can be eaten raw, cooked, sautéed, stuffed, or pickled.

Pomegranates:

The Lebanese call this the love fruit. It is even mentioned in the Kama Sutra. Today, you can buy the juice in bottles and add it to vodka for a great new martini. Or add to a margarita for a new twist! In its natural state, you eat only the seeds.

Potatoes:

Love spuds! Who knew? Try roasting the potatoes and adding a small amount of sour cream and a little caviar for a decadent side dish, or use baby potatoes and split them for an adorable, luscious appetizer.

Spinach:

Spinach has lots of iron for stamina for that steamy night that you have planned. Can be eaten raw, sautéed, or steamed.

Strawberries:

This fruit is succulent, sweet, and dripping with juice. It is the perfect bite for between your lips or hers. They go great with chocolate or champagne.

Truffles:

(Not the chocolate kind.) A truffle is a musky-smelling cousin of the mushroom. Although expensive, truffles add a unique flavor that reeks of sex! Sometimes you can find oil infused with truffles to drizzle over mashed potatoes.

Watermelon:
Also has Viagra-like effects. It is cold, wet, sweet, and juicy all in one bite. Now you know why you should have it at your next barbeque!

Kiwi, celery, and pineapple are also supposed to sweeten the flavor of her vaginal secretions!

SPICES, HERBS, AND SEEDS

Basil:
Basil was used in ancient love spells to keep wandering eyes focused homeward. Buttery green or purple leaves add flavor and fragrance. Basil oil can be applied to the skin as an aphrodisiac. Basil is best fresh, but can be easily found dried at your local market.

Chilies:
These are great as an aphrodisiac and a wonderful way to fire up your taste buds. There are over two hundred kinds of chilies, and they vary greatly in their hotness. They get your blood rushing and your face flushing, and they make you sweat. This is the reason why people in hot climates eat a lot of spicy foods. Nature's way to cool down your system is using your own sweat. You might want to check in with your partner to see if she likes and can tolerate spicy foods, or you might just fizzle out for the night while she nurses her burned mouth or stomach.

Cloves:

These are a great way to help your digestion and increase your sexual appetite. The scent will remind you of the holidays: cloves work well with pumpkin pie, ham, and sweet potato pie. You can use whole or powdered cloves depending on the recipe.

Garlic:

Gives you strength and virility. Great for your heart, which will be pumping hard as you and your partner get down to romping around! Garlic can be eaten raw, roasted, spread on bread, or sautéed in a dish. It can be found in whole heads, with the papery skin that needs to be removed before eating, dried, or prechopped in a jar. This is a staple in my kitchen!

Ginger:

Wards off impotence, soothes the stomach, and helps your blood flow to the important parts of your anatomy with oxygen rich blood. Ginger can be found in powder form, raw, or candied for use in desserts.

Mint:

Spearmint activates parts of your brain just with the smell. It also acts as an aphrodisiac. Peppermint calms an upset stomach when it is added to hot tea. Their essential oil opens up the sense of smell and enhances your ability to taste.

Nutmeg:

Has properties similar to mescaline (yes, I read this) and may help prevent premature ejaculation. It is used in pumpkin pie spices and supposedly increases blood flow to a man's privates. Happy Thanksgiving! Gobble-Gobble!

Pine Nuts:
A little kernel of love. These buttery nuts might increase fertility and a natural nesting instinct, and they make you horny! These can be eaten raw, toasted, or ground up like in pesto.

Pumpkin Seeds:
Roasted, they increase libido...feed them to each other and find out.

Rosemary:
It has an aroma that fills your senses and captivates you like a love potion. It is a great spice to add to chicken or a roasted leg of lamb.

Saffron:
Taken from the Crocus flower, they are part of the stamen (the reproductive part of the flower). They make erogenous zones more sensitive. Add a little to a rice dish where it will add color, fragrance, and make your love juices flow!

Walnuts:
These were used in Roman fertility rituals. Latin name means "glens of Jupiter." Also used in Wiccan marriage spells and are great in brownies.

SEAFOOD

Anchovies:
Italians swear that they get your love juices flowing.

Caviar:
Small, salty, bursting in your mouth, decadent, and delicious! The most well-known version from movies and lifestyles of the rich and fabulous is black caviar, which has different grades that vary widely in source and price; there is also a wide variety of colors and sources for fish eggs. Red caviar is commonly used in sushi, from large to small eggs depending on what fish it came from, and is also common in the Greek dish taramasalata. Many cultures use various kinds of caviar from different types of fish including cod and salmon.

Oysters:
You can't talk about sexy foods without mentioning oysters. Raw, they resemble a woman's genitals. Packed with protein, iron, and iodine, they are the perfect sex food. It is said that Casanova ate fifty a day! They can also be found smoked in a can, and they can be eaten raw or cooked.

Shrimp:
Although less potent than an oyster, they are powerful stimulators nonetheless. Buy frozen cooked and peeled shrimp and keep in the freezer for a quick meal.

SWEETS

Only for external usage or as a food item...do NOT use internally on your woman! (The yeast infection that will follow will kill your sex life for at least a week!) But do drizzle a little on your partner and lick it off...this includes whipped cream too. Be naughty with food just because it's fun and hot to play with.

<u>Chocolate:</u>
Besides melting in your mouth and covering your tongue with buttery sweet and bitter tastes, it releases serotonin—the feel-good hormone. Cocoa has many antioxidants and a little caffeine to get you up and keep you up and increase your blood flow into your love-craving veins. The darker the chocolate, the more cocoa is in it.

<u>Honey:</u>
This is one of the oldest love, sex, and sensuality ingredients. It has a high sugar content that converts right into energy. The drippy, sticky nectar from flowers gives sexual vigor. Honey comes in different grades; hence, some types of honey are darker than others. Some honeys are also infused with different flower essences depending on where the bees traveled, so they have an interesting variety of flavors and scents.

<u>Licorice:</u>
The smell of licorice increases blood flow to the sexual organs. Also mentioned in the Kama Sutra, it promotes sexual vigor. The after-dinner drinks ouzo and sambuca have a licorice flavor.

Marzipan:
A paste made from almonds, it is usually used in desserts or rolled into candies. Eaten before lovemaking, it increases one's desires, but don't get crumbs in the bed!

Vanilla:
Some people love the scent of vanilla in a bubble bath to turn them on. Some people love the subtle scent and flavor that it adds to desserts like custards and ice cream. It is usually found in liquid form mixed with alcohol. Only a small amount is needed to flavor food or fruit, especially strawberries.

BEVERAGES

Champagne:
Viva La France! Only real champagne is made from grapes grown in the Champagne region of France. The others are made from grapes in the champagne tradition, but cannot be called champagne. It hides under the name of a sparkling wine, but it can be just as good. Place a strawberry in the champagne glass or on the rim of the glass for a special treat and let the bubbles take you and your partner away. Sparkling cider or juice is a good replacement for those who don't drink alcohol.

Coffee:
Known to increase libido and to prolong erections, it is the breakfast of champions! Besides, you won't fall asleep on your lover.

Cognac:

If you enjoy strong liqueurs there is nothing like a warm cognac after dinner. The oaky smell wafts up your nose and opens the senses. The warm liqueur drips down your throat, and you can feel the warmth everywhere...and I mean EVERYWHERE.

Ruby Port:

Originally from Portugal, these grape-based wines have an unusual flavor. Ruby ports are wonderful with chocolate, so you get two aphrodisiacs at the same time. Letting it linger on the tongue brings out the subtle flavors of the port. It has a powerful scent that opens up your sense of smell and stimulates the brain for later.

Tawny Port:

It is rumored that this port is especially powerful when combined with strawberries.

Tequila:

The ultimate libido enhancer will get the sexual energy flowing. Do tequila shooters with salt and lime or make margaritas for a refreshing cold way to start your seduction dinner.

So, now you have the primer of the love foods. And now you can approach the kitchen with confidence and knowledge as to how to take your meal from boring to the bedroom. You might even want to grow a kitchen "love garden" and fill it with live rosemary, basil, mint, and chives so that you can enjoy fresh herbs whenever you please, or want to get pleased. Next, we'll even give you some simple recipes that utilize these ingredients so that you can cook in two places... no matter how good a cook you are.

Recipes:

Make a meal of finger foods! Feed them to each other for a sexy prelude to an even hotter night! Set out a tablecloth on the floor, in front of the fireplace if you have one, and pretend you are on a picnic! Light candles, pour a fun beverage, and take turns feeding or eating finger foods off each other for a change of pace!

Try:

- Washing whole mushrooms, cut off the stems, spray or rub them with a little olive oil, and stuff with premade soft cheese spread, some pine nuts, and sprinkle a little dill and paprika on them. Bake in an oven at 350 degrees on a baking pan for about 15 minutes until bubbly. Let cool before eating!

- Clean and cut cucumbers into ¼ inch thick slices. Spread each one with sour cream and add a little caviar on top. The contrast of cold, salty, and creamy is fabulous. You can substitute smoked salmon instead of caviar or use a pre-made smoked fish spread of your choice!

- If you can't find them fresh, soak dried figs in some tawny port. Simmer for a few minutes, which will boil out the alcohol taste. Let it cool and pour it over ice cream or put it in a bowl next to some exotic cheeses like blue cheese or Roquefort. Even a ripe Camembert-style cheese will be amazing next to the "drunken" figs!

Get Cooking With Foods That Make You Feel Sexy!

- Make a spread for bread or crackers! Take a can of cooked white beans, drain them, and place in a food processor. Add 1 tablespoon chopped garlic, a splash of olive oil, and chili pepper flakes, if you like it spicy. Sprinkle paprika on top for a pretty garnish—parsley can be used also. The more oil you use, the wetter the spread, so add a little more if it is too thick!

- Chicken on a skewer: Soak wooden skewers in water for about 15 minutes (so that they do not burn when you cook them). Take chicken tenders or slice boneless chicken breasts into 1 inch wide slices. Make sure that you cut away the fat and gristly parts. Thread the chicken onto the skewers lengthwise. Marinate in Italian dressing and sprinkle with dried rosemary and a little parmesan cheese. Bake in oven for about 15 minutes at 350 degrees until they are fully cooked, the juices are clear, and the chicken is not dried out. The same technique can also be done with skirt steak! Another easy way to marinate them is with bottled teriyaki sauce mixed with a little honey before cooking. You'll need your protein to keep up the mood for your sexy night!

Must-haves for your pantry to keep on hand for a quick meal:

Garlic (powdered or better is prechopped in oil kept in the fridge)
Rosemary
Paprika
Chili powder and/or flakes
Basil
Parsley

Mint
Ginger
Cumin
Cilantro
Pepper
Cinnamon
Nutmeg
Extra virgin olive oil
Artichoke hearts (marinated in oil or canned)
Toothpicks
Balsamic vinegar
Dried figs, dates
Walnuts, pine nuts
Canned garbanzo beans or white beans
Canned chopped tomatoes
Bottled vinaigrette salad dressing (balsamic vinaigrette
   has the most interesting flavor)
Teriyaki sauce
Honey
Chocolate sauce

When asked by radio host Kim Iverson to create a
meal that would use aphrodisiac foods, Dr. Joni (head
chef of the house) created an easy and creative sexy,
aphrodisiac-filled menu (many people were calling the
station for the recipes, so here they are):

Suggested Meal:

Pomegranate Margaritas
Shrimp Cocktail with Spicy Cocktail Sauce
Roasted Chicken with Lemon and Rosemary
Garlic Roasted Red Potatoes
Sautéed Asparagus with a Crunchy Topping
Strawberry Cream Cheese Puffs with Chocolate Sauce
Recipes: Servings are for two people

Pomegranate Margaritas

4 ounces pomegranate juice
Juice of 5 limes—keep 1 wedge for each glass
Kosher or sea salt to rim the glasses
3 ounces gold tequila
1 ounce orange liqueur (Cointreau or Grand Marnier
    or Triple Sec)
1 teaspoon sugar
Rub rim with lime wedge, put salt in shallow plate, and
    dip the rim into the salt.
Combine pomegranate juice, tequila, Cointreau, sugar,
    and shake over ice cubes.
Strain into glasses, place lime wedge over edge of
    glass and serve!

Shrimp Cocktail with Spicy Cocktail Sauce

Buy large frozen cooked shelled shrimp and defrost as instructed on package (marinate them in a little tequila for 10 minutes if desired).

Make cocktail sauce or buy bottled cocktail sauce and add hot sauce or horseradish to kick it up to your desired level of spice.

To make spicy cocktail sauce:
½ cup ketchup
2 teaspoons grated horseradish (can be bottled)
Juice of ½ a lemon
Dash Tabasco
Dash Worcestershire sauce
Combine all ingredients and mix together (can be
    made in advance)

Roasted Lemon Rosemary Chicken

Although I prefer to use a whole chicken, you can also use chicken breasts on the bone. Putting the spices under the skin gives the chicken more flavors and keeps it juicier!

1 large roasting chicken (4 – 5 lbs)
2 teaspoons paprika
2 tablespoons rosemary
1 teaspoon salt
½ teaspoon ground pepper
2 lemons
1 teaspoon olive oil
2 tablespoons flour
1 cup chicken broth
1 tablespoon lemon juice
2 teaspoons sugar

Clean chicken inside and out with water and remove excess fat. Starting at the neck side, use your fingers to loosen the skin from the breast meat and thighs.

Combine paprika, 1 tablespoon rosemary, ½ teaspoon salt, and ¼ teaspoon pepper. Rub under the loosened skin. Thinly slice lemons and arrange under skin of chicken. Cut remaining lemon into quarters and place them inside the cavity of the chicken.

Coat a roasting pan with cooking spray or a little oil and place chicken in pan. Brush chicken with oil on the outer skin. Cover with aluminum foil and bake for 30 minutes at 425 degrees. Uncover and bake another 50 minutes at 375 degrees until done. Place on cutting board and let it rest for 15 minutes.

Remove grease from drippings and place gravy in a pan on stove over medium heat. Mix flour into a small amount of gravy in a cup and add to drippings. Add wine and bring to a boil while stirring. Add broth, juice, sugar, remaining ¼ teaspoon pepper, remaining 1 tablespoon of thyme and ½ teaspoon salt to pan until thickened. Remove from heat.

Carve chicken, without skin and lemons, and serve with gravy. Garnish with a fresh lemon slice.

Garlic Roasted Potatoes

8 small red russet potatoes
¼ cup of olive oil
1 teaspoon paprika
2 teaspoon crushed or powdered garlic
½ teaspoon salt
½ teaspoon pepper

Cut potatoes into quarters, so the pieces are approximately the same size. Combine ingredients in a bowl first, add potato pieces, and toss. Pour coated potatoes into a glass baking dish and put in the oven once you take the cover off the chicken. The potatoes will be ready when you are ready to take out the chicken.

Sautéed Asparagus with Crunchy Topping

1 bunch asparagus
1 ½ tablespoons olive oil
Dash of salt and black pepper to taste

For topping:
¼ cup chopped walnuts or almonds
¼ teaspoon garlic, powdered or minced
1 tablespoon parsley
Dash of salt and black pepper

Set a large pan on the stove over high heat. Rinse asparagus well—snap off the tough ends. Drizzle with olive oil and toss to coat. Place asparagus into hot pan and season with salt and pepper. Toss several times. Cover pan and reduce heat to medium. Toss occasionally for even cooking. After about 2 minutes, throw in nuts and spices and continue to toss over the heat. Total cooking time: about 4–6 minutes.

Dessert: Strawberry Cream Cheese Puffs with Chocolate Sauce

¼ cup cream cheese at room temperature
4 tablespoons light brown sugar, divided in half
2/3 cup coarsely chopped fresh strawberries
¼ teaspoon cinnamon
One 8 count package refrigerated crescent rolls
2 tablespoons sweet cream butter, melted

Chocolate Sauce:

Your choice: Dove or similar ice cream topping soft chocolate sauce (dark chocolate is best) or use honey if chocolate is not your favorite.

Preheat oven to 375 degrees.

Get Cooking With Foods That Make You Feel Sexy!

Blend the cream cheese, 2 tablespoons of the brown sugar, and cinnamon in a bowl. Gently stir in the strawberries. Unfold the crescent roll dough into four rectangles. Smooth the dough together along the diagonal dotted line. Divide the strawberry cream cheese mixture among the four pieces, spooning onto the bottom half of the rectangle. Fold the dough over and pinch the edge together with your fingers or the tines of a fork. Place on a nonstick cookie sheet or pan and bake for 10–12 minutes or until golden brown. Brush puffs with melted butter and dust with remaining brown sugar before serving. Drizzle with chocolate sauce or honey as preferred. Enjoy!

*You can make these earlier in the day and keep them in the refrigerator until you are ready to bake them so that they are nice and hot when served.

For more recipes to turn you both on, check out our favorite cookbook, *If Food Is Love...Cooking is Foreplay* by Jim Kar. You can find it at www.iffoodislove.com.

So get cooking and get ready to take dessert into the bedroom!

Part Three: How Do Women Work—Really

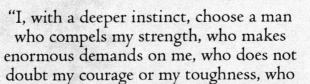

"I, with a deeper instinct, choose a man who compels my strength, who makes enormous demands on me, who does not doubt my courage or my toughness, who does not believe me naive or innocent, who has the courage to treat me like a woman."

—Anais Nin, author

CHAPTER 6.

**From Bitch In The Boardroom To Slut In The Bedroom—
Today's Woman And The Tightrope She Walks**

Today's woman: sometimes she is a contradiction in terms. Simultaneously, she needs to be several different personalities that are usually exactly the opposite of each other, and she needs to compartmentalize and separate these personalities so she can whip them out on command, depending on each situation as it presents itself. If it sounds exhausting, let us assure you right now, you are absolutely right. Women are professional jugglers: we are boardroom bitches, affectionate mothers, doting spouses, and electrifying sex goddesses rolled into one tired ball. Sometimes we run out of steam—and you may not realize why. Here's a funny voyeuristic peek into the female mind and why these personalities have trouble playing nicely together.

The Boardroom Bitch

OK, you know her—she's tough, she's demanding, she's aggressive and she gets the job done. Of course, all of these qualities are rewarded in you and in her male counterparts at the office, but she's a woman with these characteristics, so she's labeled a bitch. This is a bitter pill to swallow for most women, so it's no surprise that she may occasionally become a bitch. Remember, she's not only gotten it all done, she also got a dose of grief for being good at her job, so have a little mercy on her moods.

The Affectionate Mom

Whether she's up late sewing a pumpkin costume, comforting a little one after a nightmare, or baking cookies for junior's classmates, this mom rivals your own in her attention and care. Nothing is a bigger or more thankless job than child rearing, and she is guaranteed to be exhausted at the end of the day—whether she works outside of the house too or full time at home.

> ✹ **The bigger role you play in raising your kids, the sexier your kids' mom will find you. Nothing turns a woman on more than watching her husband play and bond with his children.**

The Doting Spouse

You love her—that's the woman who's got a beautiful dinner in the oven and remembered to pick up your lucky blazer at the dry cleaners after working all day herself. She is capable of doing several different things simultaneously like running errands while planning tonight's menu, mentally creating an agenda for a morning meeting, and deciding on a birthday present for your mother. And she never forgets to make you feel good too—she strokes your ego and makes sure that you feel loved. All this mental and physical work is draining—she's great, but this gal has usually run out steam by the time her vixen sister wants to come out and play.

The Electrifying Sex Goddess

Make no mistake—we believe every woman has this sister inside her, it's just up to you to encourage her to come out and play. This fire-breathing passion princess wants to rock your world, and she wants you to rock hers! You may have seen her the last time you were on vacation, just the two of you: a little sun, an afternoon cocktail, and the soft ocean breeze tend to bring this vixen out of hiding. Bring this woman out to play more often, and your lives, and your relationship will change forever—for the better.

So is it any wonder that women are exhausted by the end of the day? How can you, her intimate erotic friend, help her walk this tightrope and make your relationship stronger? Here are a few ideas:

Take a little off her plate

We've mentioned this before. Whether that means taking on more of the household chores, cooking occasionally, or taking over as lead parent for a couple of hours, any attempt to help her with her endless "to do" list will win you big points. Cutting down on her work load may leave her more energy, so you can encourage the vixen to come out and play!

Serious About Lightening Her Load: Try This Homework Assignment

If you're serious about taking on more of the responsibility of making your family life run smoothly, but you're unsure of how to move forward, try this easy division of chores list. Don't obsess over the past. Use this list as a way to redesign your present and your future. Decide together which tasks each of you are willing to do, and reassign those chores accordingly. Start with the things you like to do, and progress to things you can live with. Any pressure you take off her will be a welcome change, and consistent behavior over time will show her that your intention is to play full tilt, a recommitment to the success of your family.

Add or subtract chores from this list as they apply to you and your family. As with everything, take what you need and leave the rest.

Household:
Laundry: Doing it ___ Me ___ You ___ Together
Folding it ___ Me ___ You ___ Together
Putting it ___ Me ___ You ___ Together
away

Food shopping:
Doing it ___ Me ___ You ___ Together
Putting it ___ Me ___ You ___ Together
all away

Food Preparation:
(Take In or Going out can count for your turn - as long as the usual chef has the night off.)
Dinners:
Monday ___ Me ___ You ___ Together
Tuesday ___ Me ___ You ___ Together
Wednesday ___ Me ___ You ___ Together
Thursday ___ Me ___ You ___ Together
Friday ___ Me ___ You ___ Together
Saturday ___ Me ___ You ___ Together
Sunday ___ Me ___ You ___ Together

* Add breakfasts and lunches to your list if you work from home or have some time off together. And remember, a surprise breakfast in bed never sent anyone to the doghouse!

Cleaning Chores:

Vacuuming ___ Me ___ You ___ Together
Moping ___ Me ___ You ___ Together
Cleaning ___ Me ___ You ___ Together
the kitchen
Taking out ___ Me ___ You ___ Together
the trash
Recycling ___ Me ___ You ___ Together
Mowing ___ Me ___ You ___ Together
the lawn
Washing ___ Me ___ You ___ Together
the car(s)
Pool Care ___ Me ___ You ___ Together

Child Care:

Getting them ___ Me ___ You ___ Together
up in the morning
Getting them ___ Me ___ You ___ Together
ready for
school/ daycare
Making their ___ Me ___ You ___ Together
Breakfasts
Preparing ___ Me ___ You ___ Together
their lunches
Taking them ___ Me ___ You ___ Together
to school/daycare
Picking ___ Me ___ You ___ Together
them up
Homework ___ Me ___ You ___ Together
Patrol
Play time ___ Me ___ You ___ Together
Bath time ___ Me ___ You ___ Together
Bedtime ___ Me ___ You ___ Together
Stories
Putting them ___ Me ___ You ___ Together
down to sleep

*As necessary, recreate this list to include doctor's appointments, sports practice, band rehearsal, dentist visits, the principal's office, etc. You can also implement different chore rotation on different days, like taking turns preparing lunches or picking the kids up. Remember, divide and conquer is your motto.

Design this list as it applies to your family, and post it on the fridge every week. It will keep you both on plan and help avoid duplication or the blame game if someone slips up. Posting it also helps keep your busy lives in order. Remember, a balanced family is a happy family!

We know this exercise looks a little daunting, and for some of you, colorful language and cursing under your breath is your automatic response, with a "what do you mean I have to cook and do laundry?!" This is not a setup for your partner to say "Look at all that I do, while you don't do anything!" Don't panic; this list is just a suggestion, and it gives you a sneak peek into the long list of chores that it takes to make your family and home run smoothly. Here's a great reason to consider taking on more home-based responsibilities: by lightening her load, maybe both of you will have more time and energy for sex more often. Besides, nothing turns a woman on more than a man who's willing to do chores! (This is especially true when you choose to do them without having to be asked.) Give it a shot and find out for yourself if it works!

🦋 Verbal Appreciation Goes A Long Way
Compliments are easy, free and a great way to make your lover feel sexy, as long as they're genuine. Women need to feel appreciated, it makes us feel like all the work we do is worth it. When

women feel appreciated, we feel loved. When women feel loved, we feel sexy. When women feel sexy, we want to have sex. Bingo—you just heard the reason why compliments are the fastest and easiest way to leading to a more fulfilling sex life!

Commit to Couple Time

No one is suggesting that you send the kids to Grandma and go on a six-month cruise around the world. That said, it is your duty to each other to take time for you as a loving couple. It could be a couple of hours at a coffee shop, a romantic dinner, a weekend away from home, or a week in the sun while grandparents take over. The length of time or amount of money you spend isn't important, but the quality of the time you spend together is. Walk holding hands, reconnect physically and emotionally—so you can reconnect and revitalize sexually. (Remember our motto—Vacation Sex is Best!)

*If you're worried about twangs of parental guilt, studies have shown that kids learn about what it means to be in love from watching you. Would you rather they think that marriage is about crashing and burning after putting the kids to bed, about arguing over money and chores, or would you prefer to have them wonder about the lock on your bedroom door and the giggling they hear late at night? Romantic love is the best lesson you can teach your kids, so they learn from experts what kind of relationship they want when it's their turn.

Encourage the Vixen to Come Out and Play

You know, it's different for guys. It's usually much easier for you to get in the mood, and stay there. For women, it can take more work. The work starts in our heads—hence the compliments section above. It continues on a physical level, since women need a lot more "priming of the pump" so to speak, to get our bodies to the peak of arousal. But never forget the payback for all this effort—women are designed to be multiorgasmic, so the longer you please her, the more fun she is guaranteed to have. And the more fun she has, the more often this sex goddess is going to want to make an appearance in your bedroom (or any other room of the house for that matter!) Sex has so many benefits—it's good for your health, it helps you sleep better, it decreases stress, and it feels so damn good. Celebrate your sexuality together and you will find that your sex goddess will be tempted to make more regularly scheduled visits.

Decide to Become Love Warriors

We are all tired at the end of the day, and maybe striving for daily sex is an unrealistic goal. But here's a thought—consider taking on one of our challenges at www.LoveHerRight.com and commit to having sex daily for a specific period of time. If you haven't already read it, check out Doug Brown's great book, *Just Do It – How One Couple Turned Off The TV And Turned On Their Sex Lives For 101 Days (No Excuses!)*. It's a really fun read, and it's the inspiration for our Love Warrior Challenge. By incorporating sex into your daily list of things you must do, like brushing your teeth or daily exercise, you are making sex a priority in your lives and telling your bodies to take you down new paths of pleasure. You are also forcing your relationship to function on a much higher and more passionate level, which translates into your relationship taking on a new level of importance and priority in your life. You will be amazed at how your world transforms, when you both begin living with more passion, and demanding it. Seduction and the art of making love are always a work in progress. How much more enjoyable could a life's work be than exploring how to bring your partner to new heights of sexual pleasure? Take on one of these challenges, and find out just how amazing life can become when the vixen moves in to stay.

CHAPTER 7.
Your Brain On Love: The Chemical Cocktail Shaker

We have spoken to psychiatrists, psychologists, and now a neuroscience researcher, and they all have a debate about what gives us the ability to love, feel lust, and how we enter into a romantic relationship. They talk about Dr. Freud, Carl Jung, and others and have linked our psychological makeup to plenty of topics that usually lead us back to square one. Maybe they all have parts of it right. But, maybe some of it has to do with how our brain develops in the first place. The better question is, why should you care?

Well, we'll give you a good reason. The human brain is a chemical cocktail shaker of sorts. Using brain chemicals that we produce, the brain reacts to whatever stimulates it, if we have created the parts to receive the messages in the first place. The second good reason is that we can increase our abilities to receive these messages, no matter what age we are, in order to have more loving, trusting relationships! We can undo anything that has kept us from loving fully and learn to embrace love and trust with a little work. How? By learning about a chemical called oxytocin—our new brain chemical friend that allows us to trust, cuddle, love, and orgasm!

Dr. Joni: Oxytocin is not to be confused with the controversial addictive drug OxyContin. It wouldn't be a bad thing to become addicted to high levels of oxytocin—you will be naturally very loving and lovable!

Our favorite book on this topic is called *The Chemistry Of Connection* by Susan Kuchinskas, and we are so grateful for her wisdom and insight into actual scientific data concerning the love connection and brain chemistry.

What You Never Learned in Biology Class and Are Going To Wish You Did!

Let's start with the basics. Men and women possess several important hormones that also function as brain chemicals: estrogen, testosterone, prolactin, adrenaline, noradrenaline, cortisol, vasopressin, and oxytocin. How much of each chemical we produce and how they all combine in our bodies is what separates the genders, and every individual will have different levels of these chemicals at any given time. We all have the ability to create our new friend, oxytocin, and both men and women release a burst of oxytocin during orgasm. How oxytocin combines in our bodies is different for men and women, evoking different emotional responses.

Ever notice how women want to cuddle after making love and men want to sleep or get out of bed? Here's why: for women, oxytocin combines with estrogen, making her want to bond and cuddle. Men respond *very* differently. When a man climaxes, his brain also produces vasopressin, which puts his body on alert and may increase anxiety. Because men have a proportionally higher amount of testosterone than women, and because **testosterone diminishes the bonding effects of oxytocin**, men don't feel like cuddling after sex; they want to get up and go work on the car or tinker on their favorite project. Men also produce norepinephrine, which is the chemical that puts you on watch guard duty. It is also called the fight or flight response. It keeps men away from situations that don't feel comfortable, or it may be released if the man is excited or interested in something or someone. (If you've ever had a one-night stand and leaped out of bed afterward because you felt like you just HAD to get out of there—that's norepinephrine!) Here's the real kicker: it seems that women need the oxytocin *first* in order to trust a man enough to want to have sex with him...hmmmm. (Remember, oxytocin is about bonding.) Men, conversely need orgasm to release enough of a boost of oxytocin to even get close to feeling like bonding.

We think that this combination of brain chemicals helps to clarify why women need to feel safe and secure before they can commit to a relationship and have sex. It also helps us to understand why men feel the need to have sex first before letting down their guard in order to commit to the woman. Here is the clear breakdown of the different phases of love and how the brain chemicals interact by the different genders in order to have a fulfilling, long-lasting love relationship.

1) Lust

This is what we've been talking about so far. Lust is the drive for sex, and oxytocin is a key player. During the lust phase, men need oxytocin in order to achieve and maintain an erection. Oxytocin is released in large quantities during female and male orgasm. For women, oxytocin is the brain chemical of trust and bonding. At orgasm, her huge dose of oxytocin bonds with her estrogen, and this drives her to want to bond emotionally (that's why she wants to cuddle after sex!) in order to evaluate whether she wants to enter into the next phase of a relationship: Romance.

2) Romance

During romance, the brain chemicals change a bit as the relationship shifts to wanting to have an emotional union, not just sex. In addition to estrogen and testosterone, the human brain also releases dopamine, a feel-good hormone, mixed with norepinephrine and serotonin to make an intoxicating brain cocktail. That's why women and men feel that wild, crazy, out of control feeling during the dance of romance. Ask any teenager and they'll remind you what wild crazy obsessive hormone-driven attraction looks like. The problem with adolescents is that their bodies are saying one thing, even though their brains are not ready for true commitment. The cocktail shaker is overwhelmed with dopamine, and we feel as if we are mentally addicted to romance like a drug. The section of the brain affected is our built-in reward center, which seeks out that feeling of euphoria by continually raising the levels of dopamine being put into the mix. Luckily, the levels of serotonin actually go down and our cortisol levels go up, to stress us out and keep us from becoming completely obsessive at the same time. Confused yet? Then our brain chemistry changes again, as we contemplate taking the relationship to the next level: love.

3) Love

During the love phase, our brains are bonding to our partner's with the help of oxytocin and dopamine. Couples are seeking that special connection, but in a calmer fashion. This stage is where men and women actually become more compatible. Sex, while great, is no longer just about feeling good. The rewards of sex are tied to one specific partner, creating a conditioned response not unlike a long-time physical addiction. As men and women age, our hormonal levels also decrease, with her estrogen levels falling rapidly at menopause and his testosterone levels declining over several decades. This causes a slight role reversal in sex drive, but it also ensures that the effects of oxytocin are intensified for both partners, making sexually active long-term couples some of the happiest and closest couples alive.

__Making sense of all of this__

Simply put, oxytocin is responsible and necessary for two people to bond. It gives us the rush during sexual excitement and during orgasm and keeps us both calmer during conflicts and less stressed out. The circle of a happy relationship is a wonderful feeling of closeness, which creates more oxytocin. With this flood of oxytocin, couples are happier, they stay healthier, have better sex, are less stressed, and sleep better. Therefore, the combination of emotional connection, love, and physical health explains our deep need for intimacy.

Here is the ultimate kick in the pants: our brains have to be taught how to absorb this amazing bonding hormone, and our brains are not fully developed until we are three years old. That means that whatever may have happened to us as children, especially before age three, has affected us later on unless we learn how to increase our oxytocin receptors. So how can we increase our levels of oxytocin if we want to have all of these wonderful parts of a relationship? It is easier than you might think. Here's a list of oxytocin-boosting activities first published in *The Chemistry of Connection*:

How to Boost your Oxytocin levels:

1. Kiss more
2. Cuddle
3. Sing out loud, singing with others works well
4. Make love
5. Share a hug
6. Have an orgasm (alone or with someone else)
7. Give someone a neck rub
8. Hold a baby
9. Pet a dog or cat
10. Pray
11. Perform a generous act
12. Root for your favorite team

So, if you struggle with relationships, you can always have another chance to rebuild the oxytocin receptors in your brain to allow it in, and you can learn to love more deeply than you ever imagined. You can always have the power to change your love "set point" to a higher and deeper level. Keep repeating the exercises that make your brain give off more oxytocin, and your brain will retrain itself. Spark up your brain receptors and enjoy the power of oxytocin—your life will be better for it.

Please note that we are not saying that psychotherapy is not needed. Many therapists are embracing neuro-chemistry into their understanding of the brain and its relationship to psychological thinking. We believe that it takes a multidisciplinary approach to healing, and we applaud reaching out to any source that you find help-ful. Go for it!

CHAPTER 8.
Female Anatomy 101 For Real Men

Dr. Joni: Don't fall asleep or gloss over this section! This is the key to your sexy, mutually satisfying future!

This section is heavily influenced by a similar section in *The Ultimate Guide to Cunnilingus—How to Go Down on A Woman and Give Her Exquisite Pleasure* by Violet Blue. This book is an incredible resource and a must-have for your sexual "how to" library, and we are grateful for Violet's excellent work. Since her descriptions of female anatomy are wonderfully accurate and in layman's terms, we have borrowed and abridged her work here in order to give you a basic understanding of how women are built and how their parts work without reinventing the wheel. Brace yourself: this is not anything you learned in the locker rooms of your youth.

(We suggest that if you are reading this book together, you may want to do a visual inspection of your lover after reading this section.) With this description fresh in your mind, you can test your knowledge and see how each part of her reacts to your touch. Beware that all of her is VERY sensitive, so a very light touch please, and let's start small—fingers only for now. If you are not reading this book together, please read the entire book and complete the recommended suggestions in each section in order before trying to show off your newly acquired sexual knowledge. Once you're ready to try a few of our techniques, you may find it helpful to reread this section on anatomy before taking the plunge, just to be sure you have the road map to heaven clearly imprinted on your mind!

Your woman's pleasure zone is situated at the rolling hill of flesh over the pubic bone, which is usually covered with hair. The amount of hair, much like every aspect of a woman's body that we will discuss, varies greatly from one individual to the next. Some women leave their hair naturally wild, some tailor their pubic hair with shaving or waxing, and some prefer to be clean shaven. The first parts that you will notice are the outer lips, or labia of the vagina. Since they are on the outside of the body, they are usually the same color, or somewhat darker than the surrounding skin, and covered with hair on the outer surface and are smooth and free from hair on the inner surface. Their appearance ranges from person to person from puffy and fleshy to thin and flat. Vive la difference!

As you begin to explore your lover's body and separate these lips, you will observe a second set of lips that surround the vaginal opening. This is the inner labia, and their texture is much like the lips you love to kiss on her face. They can also vary greatly in shape, size, and color, and usually no two are alike. One lip is usually bigger than the other, and their appearance can change after childbirth. These lips are full of rich and sensitive nerve endings, and many women find their stimulation as good as or better than direct clitoral stimulation. These lips meet in two corners: toward the anus at the perineum (the wall separating the vagina and the anus) and toward the pubic bone, where they form a protective hood that covers the clitoris. Just above the clitoris is the clitoral shaft, similar to the shaft of your penis. Although it is hard to see, you can feel it like a tubular cord that can get erect with stimulation. Many women get turned on by stroking the clitoral shaft before direct clitoral contact. Some women cannot tolerate direct clitoral contact due to the enormous amount of nerve endings in the clitoris, so stimulating the shaft or the outer labia is a great alternative. (You will want to start slowly, to determine how sensitive she is. We'll discuss this in detail when we talk about techniques in later chapters.)

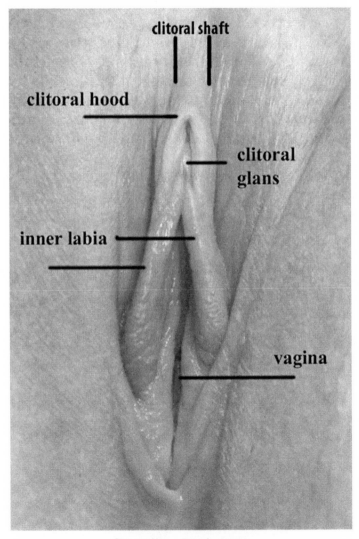

clitoral shaft

clitoral hood

clitoral glans

inner labia

vagina

©Heather Buchanan

Before we go on, let's discuss the realities of sensitivity. Every woman is different. What feels good to one may not feel as good to another.

Dr. Joni: And her time of the month may change her needs!

Many women prefer to be stimulated around the clitoris instead of direct play because it may be too sensitive to be enjoyable. The perineum, that little section between her vagina and the anus, is very sensitive for many women and a fabulous teaser when looking for arousal whether using tongue or touch. Again, please remember that softer works better than harder stimulation until you know what your partner prefers when it comes to pressure and friction. She will guide you along until you both strike the right tempo in order to have her achieve an orgasm.

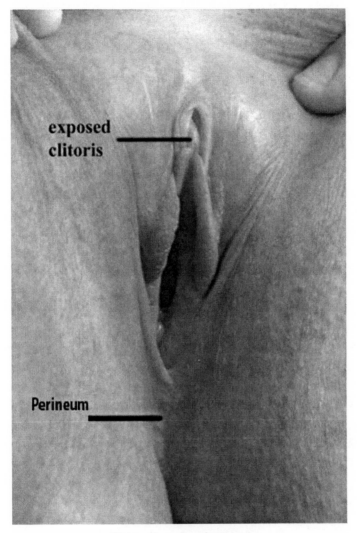

©Heather Buchanan

The clitoris is going to become the focus of all of your lovemaking efforts, or very near to it. Why? According to another wonderful resource, *The Clitoral Truth* by Rebecca Chalker, there are about 8,000 nerve endings in the small clitoris, which is about the size of a pea, and all of them send pleasure messages to the brain. **Not only does the**

clitoris have more nerve endings than any other part of the human body, male or female (twice as many as the entire penis), its only job is to provide pleasure. This amazing body part does nothing else and is usually essential in a woman's ability to reach orgasm. As we have discussed, touching it directly can be almost uncomfortable and painful to some, so it is a good thing that there is a protective hood, analogous to a man's foreskin. The hood also diffuses the sensations, although some women prefer even less direct contact, like the surrounding lips. Remember: each woman is different. The top corner of the inner lips comes to an "A" shape underneath a jacket of flesh that covers the tip of the clitoris, also called the glans. Glans means "a small round mass or body" and "tissue that can swell or harden." The entire covering of the clitoris is called the hood, and hoods range in appearance much like the inner lips. To expose the clitoris, you may be able to pull back the tip of the hood, or you may not be able to see it at all until she is aroused. The glans is nestled under the hood and also varies in size and grows upon arousal, as does the entire clitoral shaft, as it is made up of erectile tissue. Unlike the penis, there are no muscles that compress the blood flow to retain stiffness, which may explain why women are capable of being multiorgasmic. (We'll bet that you didn't know that women "get hard" too!)

What you should also know is that the tiny tip of the clitoris that you may be able to see is only the tip of the iceberg. As the captain of the Titanic can tell you, never underestimate how much of the iceberg lies beneath the surface. The enormous amount of muscles, tissue, connecting nerves, and ligaments inside the clitoris all react and engage when your partner is turned on. Pressure from dilated clitoral blood vessels inside the vagina forces clear liquid through the walls of the vagina, and at the opening of the vagina, which is where the majority of vaginal lubrication comes from through small ducts. Be aware that the amount of lubrication is also an arena where women differ and can be due to a host of things, like hormone levels, medications, stress level, or arousal level. As she becomes more aroused, the symphony of all of these muscles and ligaments contracting and the simultaneous constant firing of all of these nerve endings leave her begging for more. All of her body is more sensitive now—her hands, feet, breasts, lips, etc. Don't forget to touch and use your mouth on these areas too. At the pinnacle of her arousal, the muscular tension explodes in a series of short, rhythmic contractions throughout the muscles in the vagina and on the pelvic floor, causing intense pleasure. This is what she was waiting for—the famous, fabulous, mind-blowing clitoral orgasm, and she may be able to continue to come numerous times, either using the same technique or incorporating others. Many women enjoy having oral and manual stimulation at the same time for combined clitoral and G-Spot orgasms!

Esther: I blame the complete misunderstanding about women's sexual anatomy on our American puritanical culture. Because we have all been taught that sex is only about procreation and that the sexual organs are a penis and a vagina, we have been led to believe that no other parts are involved. What if instead we had been taught about the penis and the clitoris and, by the way, there's also a place to put that penis while you're in the neighborhood, but you'd better ask the clitoris permission first? Everyone's early sexual experiences would have been dramatically different, don't you think? Imagine being taught that sex could be about just pleasure for both partners. Talk about a sexual revolution!

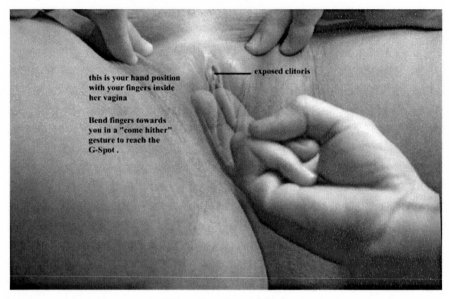

this is your hand position
with your fingers inside
her vagina

Bend fingers towards
you in a "come hither"
gesture to reach the
G-Spot .

exposed clitoris

©Heather Buchanan

Now here is another news flash: the G-Spot does exist, and you can actually give your lover the ability to ejaculate. Yes, ejaculate. Bet you thought that was only a stunt in porn movies, huh? (A cool recommendation is an instructional DVD called "The G-Spot and Female Ejaculation," available on our store Web site, www.LoveHerRightStore. com. It shows, using six different couples, how easy it is to explore this advanced sexual technique.) When a woman ejaculates, it is not urine, although it comes out from the urethra. Both women and men have an identical ring of spongy erectile tissue surrounding the urethra (where urine leaves the body). Located on the front wall of the vagina, toward the belly button, about two inches inside, this ring is the famous G-Spot, which is an integral part of the clitoral system. During arousal, the spongy tissue becomes swollen and hard and can be touched by inserting a finger or two and stroking with a "come hither" motion. Don't dig in too hard. Some women are uncomfortable with this technique because it can feel like the bladder is being stimulated, giving her a sensation that she has to pee. This is a false message, and proper G-Spot stimulation can lead to mind-numbing orgasms. During this type of orgasm, some women may ejaculate a clear fluid from this spongy tissue. Similar to prostatic fluid, the amount released varies person to person. While many find this exotic to say the least, the ability for a woman to ejaculate takes only a little play and a sense of adventure. We will discuss this in detail later on, when we talk about technique in the coming sections.

If you and your partner have never experienced a G-Spot orgasm, you may need a little help in finding the right area to stimulate. Try one of our favorite products: Intimate Organics Discover G-Spot Stimulating Gel. Their unique formula includes certified organic extracts, Japanese peppermint oil, and L-arginine. This combination increases the size and sensitivity of the G-Spot, making it easier to find. Intimate Organics **does not** use menthol, since synthetic menthol (which is most commonly used in personal products) can be irritating and drying to a woman's clitoris and vagina. The Discover Gel comes with a guide...a road map to help you find what you're looking for! You can find this product, along with the whole line of Intimate Organics products, at our store site.

This is an overview to give you an idea of what happens when you touch different parts of her genitalia, an area we are sure, before now, was a little foreign to you. If you would like a more in-depth discussion of the female anatomy and how it works upon arousal, please read *The Ultimate Guide to Cunnilingus* by Violet Blue or *The Clitoral Truth* by Rebecca Chandler. Both are excellent resources and great additions to your library. We also recommend *The Multi-Orgasmic Couple* by Mantak and Maneewan Chia and Douglas and Rachel Abrams, MD.

CHAPTER 9.
Getting Ready To Get Sexy!

PLEASE NOTE: The techniques we begin to discuss in this section are for the monogamous, fluid-bonded couple. That means that these are not safer sex techniques unless you include a fluid barrier, such as dental dams for oral sex play on her or condoms for intercourse and for oral play on him. This may also include using rubber gloves for vaginal and anal play. Also, there are nonlatex versions of fluid barriers in case of an allergy to latex, which occurs in about thirty percent of all people. If either of you has any concerns about your sexual history, or you have not been in this monogamous relationship for ten years or more, please consider using safer sex techniques. Preventing the spread of sexually transmitted diseases is your duty as a partner and as a member of the human race. Please visit your physician to get HIV tested and tested for other sexually transmitted diseases. Please take that responsibility seriously.

Before you begin setting the stage for a romantic seduction that leads to mind-blowing lovemaking for you both, several preparations will ensure a great time. This especially applies to those of you that are uncomfortable or unfamiliar with performing oral sex on a woman. Let's get started.

General Hygiene

For those of you unfamiliar with the wonderful array of scents and tastes that make up your partner, the prospect of putting your face and mouth "down there" might be intimidating. Let us assure you, all the crap you heard in the locker rooms of your youth about girls tasting or smelling like fish are nonsense. Nothing is further from the truth. What you may find interesting and something to keep tabs on is that every woman will taste and smell different depending on where she is in her menstrual cycle, what medications she may be taking, and her diet. (For foods that change the flavor of yours and her fluids, please see our chapter on foods that make you feel sexy.) What you will discover is that every woman tastes different, and the more aroused she gets, the tastes will change. It is an incredible experience, sharing this intimate aspect with your partner, and something you will develop a craving for.

A nice place to start for every couple is to think about washing up before engaging in sexual activity. A quick shower is fine if you're in a hurry, but nothing beats a dip in a hot tub together or a bubble bath. If you can take your shower or bath together, that's even better. It's easy to feel sexy when the jets in your hot tub are swirling the water, or when you are surrounded by a mountain of sexy bubbles. (Just be sure you don't add bubble bath to a tub with jets—your bathroom will be overflowing with bubbles!) Remember, one of your goals is to get clean and fresh, but your primary goal is to bring you both to a place of feeling sexy and relaxed. When your woman feels sexy, it's a short trip to being in the mood.

Dr. Joni: Kissing her on the lips while two soapy bodies are touching is a mad turn-on! Just wait until later, when we tell you about our favorite products and positions for "Sex In The Shower"...talk about wanting to get wet!

Esther: If you are expecting any oral play from your partner, you had better be clean down there too! Nothing is a bigger turnoff than smelly, sweaty balls or skid marks on your underwear. If you are uncircumcised, be sure to wash thoroughly under the foreskin. Even if you are using an unlubricated or flavored condom for oral sex—which you must to prevent STDs unless you are a fluid-bonded couple—cleanliness is mandatory if you want to have your partner ever perform oral sex again! One bad experience is all it takes to make sure she won't want to repeat it!

Other aspects of hygiene need to be discussed. All women and men have hair around and on their genital area. How much hair she has is as individual as her fingerprint. To avoid strays catching in the back of your throat (don't laugh—it happens, and nothing is as distracting as you beginning to choke to death!), while you are washing up, run your fingers through her hair down there and you will eliminate those nasty strays. Be sure that you've already been touching each other and made your way down her body and ended up between her legs—no jumping the gun and just putting your hands down there uninvited.

Some women like to tame their personal jungle with anything from shaving to waxing. Some couples make this beauty treatment a joint venture, with you doing the trimming and shaping. This is an intimate act that can be entertaining and fun, and it requires incredible communication between you. If this is something you are interested in you have to be comfortable together and be willing to discuss it. Beware of shaving down there! The hair is coarse. When it grows back, it can be sharp. Shaving may make her itch, and the regrowth can give your face razor burn. (She can minimize this by shaving in the direction of the hair growth rather than against it. It will cut down on the possibility of ingrown hairs, which gives way to the little bumps that itch, and the regrowth may not be as sharp.) Waxing can be painful, and she must find an experienced professional. Over time, the area gets accustomed to the waxing process, and the hair will grow back thinner, and the skin will become less sensitive. Some women love the feeling of little or no pubic hair, as it gives them stimulation indirectly all of the time. Another alternative is to trim the hair with manicure scissors; this avoids the razor burn and the pain of waxing. Cream depilatories work well, but use one for sensitive skin. It's a good place to start. See what she is willing to do and what turns you both on.

As I'm sure you know, she is not the only one with body hair. Do you have any "manscaping" to do? Maybe she likes the burly curls on your chest, but what about the hair on your back or in your ears or nose? Take a moment to notice these things the next time you step out of the shower. And most important: your face. The face she loves to stroke with her fingertips and kiss with her soft lips. This is the face you are going to be resting between her legs, where her skin is as soft as her face, and just as delicate. Are you clean shaven? Is your face soft? Do you have any razor stubble? Beware that any discomfort will distract her, and that is the LAST THING that you want. So, if you have the chance, run a razor over those cheeks. Maybe try a facial moisturizer. It is sexy and manly to have skin she will love to pet!

If you are going to be touching the woman you love in her most intimate places, you had better be gentle, loving, and soft! Do yourself a favor right now: look at your hands. Is the skin on your palms and fingertips rough or dry? Are your nails clean and trimmed with no jagged edges that can catch on hair or delicate skin?

Test: If you rub your hand over her panties (or anything she's wearing that is silky if you're not invited down there yet), and your skin or nails don't get caught on the fabric, then you hands pass the test! If not, find some hand cream and a nail file before you go exploring.

You must remember that she is delicate. Her skin is thin and easily broken in the genital area, and it is filled with thousands of nerve endings. Any discomfort is magnified by these nerve endings and can send her right out of her erotic experience and into a painful one. Your hands are the deliverers of your love. Make sure they are worthy of touching the goddess of your dreams. How about those toes? Do you look like a three-toed sloth with claws? You don't want to be sliding your legs together and have your claws grab her in the middle of an ecstatic moment. Do yourself a favor and cut those claws and use hand cream regularly!

You will also be using another important body part: your mouth. Be sure your breath is fresh and teeth are clean. Beware of mouthwashes: many of them contain alcohol, which will burn her, inside and out. Mints are hazardous too, since many contain sugar, which can lead to yeast infections. Some strong mints will also give her a burning sensation…not in a sexy way. Just brush your teeth and sip your wine or water, and you'll be all set. Make sure that you do not have gum disease because you can give that to your partner too.

<u>Lubrication</u>

In much the same way that no two women have the same eye color or fingerprint, they do not have the same level of natural lubrication. How much fluid gets secreted through the vaginal wall can vary based on what time of the month it is, how much stress she is under, and what medications she may be taking. One day she may be very wet with just a whisper of what you're planning to do to her; another day, she may be dry even during oral sex. Menopause is also a major cause of lack of lubrication for many women. The point is this: oral sex can help with lubrication, since the saliva in your mouth will make her external sex organs wet. As far as internally, there are many water-based lubricants on the market. Please stay away from anything sugar based. Sugar leads to yeast, and a yeast infection will halt your sex life for at least a week, maybe two, and hurts like hell for her! Common culprits include honey, whipped cream, chocolate sauce, and anything else you can think up that includes sugar. Some commercial lubricants that have flavors also have sugar, so read the labels before you purchase. You can use chocolate and sugar-based product on the outside of her body, for breast play or cunnilingus, if you are careful and if she showers or washes up afterward. If she uses something sweet and sticky on you, be sure to wash up before intercourse. For a great selection of safe and sugar-free lubricants, please visit our store site. **Our favorite lube: Intimate Organics Hydra.** It's odorless, colorless, water based, with an almost undetectable flavor, certified organic, and vegan. It's also close to her own natural pH balance, so it works well with her body naturally. Try it! You'll never want to use anything else!

A Few Words of Caution

Nonoxynal-9

Most lubricated condoms today use this spermicidal cream. While it does kill sexually transmitted diseases, including the HIV virus, nonoxynal-9 has a few drawbacks. It is an irritant, so it becomes abrasive for your partner, inside and out. This abrasive quality can begin the breakdown of cells, which can make it easier for her to develop infections and be susceptible to STDs. Nonoxynal-9 also tastes nasty. You DO NOT want to be going down on her after having intercourse using a lubricated condom. As long as you are a fluid-bonded couple and have no need to block bodily fluids from one another, there should be no need for using this spermicide. We suggest nonlubricated condoms for oral sex play because of this, and they come in several flavors for fun and variety. If you are trying to prevent pregnancy using spermicides, please perform your oral play before intercourse prior to using condoms or before she inserts her diaphragm, if that applies. (If you're looking for a great brand of condoms that allow for amazing sensitivity and stay on no matter how wild you are, try One Condoms. We have it on great authority from our product testers that these are the best condoms on the market.)

*Since you are creating the best mutually satisfying sexual experience for you both, it is your responsibility to be sure your partner is sufficiently turned on before you progress to the next step. **She must climax first before intercourse—no negotiating on this point.** Having her climax first, before intercourse, is a way to ensure a longer, richer, and more fulfilling sexual experience for you both, for each encounter you have. Never forget that she has the potential to be multiorgasmic. If you are older than seventeen, your ability to be multiorgasmic is probably difficult, to say the least, but not impossible, as we will talk about later. But, by focusing on her first, she builds the sexual excitement for you both, and nothing is sexier than watching her come, over and over again!

Dr. Joni: Here's a tip: If you are concerned that you will be too overly excited to put her needs first, you might want to consider masturbating before your evening begins. This way, you can prevent premature ejaculation, and work up to another orgasm together.

The Laundry List

Do you or your partner have certain acts or positions that are strictly off limits? Many people do because we all have histories. An astronomical number of women, and men, have been sexually assaulted and/or sexually abused as children, and those memories don't go away. You have to be sensitive to this possibility because, depending on how your partner has dealt with these issues, there are going to be certain things that will never be comfortable for her, no matter how wonderful you are. FINE. Scratch those things from your romantic repertoire. The truth is that there is hope. **All people, regardless of their experiences, can enjoy a rich and passionate sexual life**. What everyone needs most is an understanding partner who loves him or her enough to be gentle, loving, and capable of creating a safe space for each to embrace sexuality and enjoy it. This is about safety and trust, which are core to your relationship as a whole. Be the man you know you can be, and help her to celebrate her sexuality and share it with you. Show her how safe she truly is, and she may surprise you both!

Pillow Talk

The biggest part of becoming a better lover and creating the sex life you want with your partner is to become a better communicator. You need to establish open lines of communication during every aspect of your romantic interlude—before, during, and after making love. Encourage your woman to be more verbal. Ask her what she likes, if what you are doing feels good…ask her to offer direction, like a little to the left, or harder or softer, faster or slower. Encourage her to show you—watching her give herself pleasure is thrilling and a huge turn-on for you both! And, it is instructional. Now you will see firsthand where to touch her and what she likes best. All of this is so that you can learn what turns her on. Remember, the first few times you make love after reading this are fact-finding missions. If you're lucky and a little adventurous, every time you make love, you will learn something new about your partner and what makes her moan in pleasure. (This is why we felt the need to talk about communication early, so you would have the closeness and comfort level necessary to achieve this level of openness with each other when you reach this point.)

Dr. Joni: Be her "boy toy" if that's what she needs. Let her do the driving for a change!

Communication is also important when it comes to how you are both feeling physically. There may be times when she doesn't feel sexy, like when she's menstruating. When she's premenstrual, anything can happen. Her body is reeling with hormonal havoc, which means her breasts might be so tender and painful that they should not be touched, even though they are probably larger than usual and inviting. Her stress level might be high, so she is easily pissed off or irritable. Her lubrication levels might be off, so she could be wetter or dryer than usual. On the other hand, she might be really horny and want you desperately. Don't be surprised if she tells you EXACTLY what she wants and where and how much. Hormones are evil little creatures that can turn the love of your life into the devil incarnate. If you learn how to listen for clues and watch her behavior more often, you can avoid being pricked by her horns and, instead, use the right tools to soothe the savage beast. Being open and flexible during sex will help to avoid disappointing sexual encounters.

Esther: Don't be shocked if once you've mended a few bridges and are a little more passionate on a regular basis that your girl's cycle will release a true sexual vixen. While certain parts of her may be too tender to touch, like her breasts, other areas might need a stronger touch than usual. Let her show you and tell you how to please her, and maybe her period won't be such an unwelcome visitor!

The other reason to work on your communication skills in the bedroom is that we change over time. As we will discuss later on in this book, our bodies go through some amazing changes as we age, and we have to make allowances for those changes to keep our sex lives red hot. For example, menopause can lead to not only decreased lubrication, it can also affect her sex drive and her genital sensitivity. Her hot flashes may make having you on top of her feel like she's being smothered by flames. Be sensitive to these changes, and you will still ensure hot passionate sex, even though she may already be on fire. During childbirth, some women have episiotomies performed to assist in releasing your bundle of joy, but this process involves cutting vital tissues and muscles in the vaginal wall. This decreases sensitivity and can make it harder for a woman to reach orgasm. Not to fear! All you need is patience and technique, and you can continue to make her eyes roll into the back of her head, no matter what.

Your biggest roadblock

Some women, for a host of reasons, do not like (or think they don't like) oral sex. This is where communication is key. Many women were raised with a lot of crap about their bodies, especially nonsense about being "unclean" or "dirty down there." There is also a "sinner" connotation given to people who perform or receive oral sex. There's no nice way to say this: **IT'S ALL BULLSHIT.** You need to be clear with her that you don't believe any of that crap, no matter where it came from. The other obstacle many women face is all the stuff they have about their bodies. "I taste bad" or "I smell bad" or "I'm too fat." Again, all bullshit. You must tell her that you have tasted and smelled her, and she is glorious...like nectar from the gods. We all have issues with our bodies; no one is perfect. The point is that you love her exactly how she is in this moment. She is the woman of your dreams. She is your complete fantasy, and you only wish that she could see what you see. Then, she would know the truth: that she is the most beautiful woman in the world, and you are lucky enough that she picked you. By encouraging her to see a new view of herself and her sexuality, you will do what no one has done before: release her inner goddess, and she will delight you both with her capacity for love and passion.

Esther: I can speak to this whole conversation about body image. I have struggled with my weight my entire adult life. I've also always been sensitive about sharing my body with lovers. Only Joni has discovered the one phrase that eliminates all of my inhibitions: "Your body is my temple." Now that's an incredible partner!

Part Four: Technique, Timing, and Touch: The Art Of Making Love To Your Woman

I

"Out of my flesh that hungers
and my mouth that knows
comes the shape I am seeking
for reason.
The curve of your waiting body
fits my waiting hand
your breasts warm as sunlight
your lips quick as young birds
between your thighs the sweet
sharp taste of limes.

Thus I hold you
frank in my heart's eye
in my skin's knowing
as my fingers conceive your warmth
I feel your stomach move against mine.

Before the moon wanes again
we shall come together.

II
And I would be the moon
spoken over your beckoning flesh
breaking against reservations
beaching thought
my hands at your high tide
over and under inside you
and the passing of hungers
attended forgotten.

Darkly risen
the moon speaks
my eyes
judging your roundness
delightful."

—Audre Lorde, "On A Night
of The Full Moon"

———————————————

CHAPTER 10.
How Women Want To Be Kissed

Did you know that most women surveyed say they determine how good a lover you are based on how good a kisser you are? The art of kissing is something that tends to dissipate through the course of a relationship...unless you refuse to allow that. When a couple first becomes intimate, they are in a period of discovery. Every taste, touch, and smell is intoxicating, and if you are doing it right, kissing is the best part of an early relationship. The secret is to rediscover kissing now, when every form of touch has become routine. Unfortunately, once a couple becomes set in their ways, one of the first things that changes is how often they kiss. When becoming intimate, and leading up to lovemaking, many of us forget about that very first act that kept us panting for more: the passionate, hot, sexy kiss, so we do it less and less.

Here is a great recommendation: Kiss her. Kiss her often. Not just on the cheek when you leave in the morning and not just a peck on the lips when you're ready to turn in at night. Practice kissing like you did when you first started kissing each other. Like you did before the first time you made love. Kiss her like you mean it. Kiss her like it's the only way you can explore her intimately, like you are Christopher Columbus, and her mouth is the New World. Kiss her the way you used to, when a kiss left her begging for another, and another. Rediscover kissing, and soon you will rediscover the original passion that made you want to do more than just kiss her. As we have already mentioned, kissing is a lost art that you must rediscover. Nowhere is that more important than in this moment. We want you to think back to the first time you ever made love with your beautiful woman: the passionate kisses, the touching, the eager exploration.

We have important information to share in regard to the art of kissing. Men and women view kissing from the start as a different entity. Men view kissing as a means to an end…a necessary connection on your way to having sex. Women judge whether they will sleep with a man by how good a kisser he really is. For a woman, kissing may be the deal breaker from the beginning of a relationship. Women enjoy kissing just for the sake of kissing, not for the possibility of a sexual encounter. She needs kissing to affirm the connection between you and to reassure her that you have a continuing interest in the relationship. Women will break up with a man they're dating who they feel is a lousy kisser. So, how do you stack up in the kissing department?

Now, guys, we know that you really care about how your woman perceives you as a lover and that you want to improve your techniques so that you and she can explore each other more fully and with greater satisfaction for both of you. Author Peg Sausville of *The Truth About How To Kiss Women* wrote a book based on her survey of hundreds of women. Her work talks about what women want and like about kissing, and the differences between when women are dating versus when they're in a relationship. The women surveyed were also clear about the importance of kissing in a relationship and that they were willing to try different styles of kissing. Never forget, women equate how well you kiss with how well you perform in bed!

So, here are some of the major dos and don'ts about kissing techniques and how women responded to the survey.

How Women Want To Be Kissed

Dos:
- Kiss her lips
- Brush your lips over hers softly
- Playfully nip with your lips
- Kiss one lip at a time
- Brush your lips over her cheeks and nose, planting little kisses as you go
- Keep it slow and gentle
- Touch her tongue gently with yours after lip kissing
- Try to match your kissing style with hers
- Kiss her during intercourse, and after intercourse
- Look deeply into her eyes during kissing
- Stroke her hair and or face while kissing
- Mix up kissing styles and techniques to get each other turned on
- Nibbling of ears is OK, if she likes it
- Watch her response! If she is backing away, try another approach

Don'ts:
- **NEVER** start kissing with your tongue
- Keep the saliva to a minimum...no sloppy, wet kissing
- No shoving your tongue down her throat
- No thrusting your tongue in and out of her mouth
- No bad breath
- No wet licking; it feels like the dog!
- No tongues in her ears! Ugh, it is like a "wet willie"!
- No hard biting

Esther: When we interviewed Peggy Sausville on our radio show, she told us about the recurring complaint many of the women she surveyed mentioned: the lizard kiss. Please don't flick your tongue in and out of her mouth like a snake—we have yet to hear of any woman who actually likes that! When you are kissing a woman's mouth, it is a totally different technique than the one you use when kissing her genitals. Treat her mouth with respect, so you get the opportunity to kiss her elsewhere!

So, we begin with kissing. Hot, passionate, sexy, and deep exploratory kisses, like the ones you had before you ever made love. Use your hands while you kiss her. Hold her face in your hands, pull back for a moment, and look into her eyes. What color are they right now? Tell her she is beautiful and mean it. Stroke her cheek tenderly with your fingertips, trace her lips with a finger, kiss her eyes, her nose, and then her lips—softly. Kiss her and run your fingers through her hair, pulling her head closer to you. Be gentle though, especially if she is tender. (Some women are more fragile than others and don't like to be pulled and pushed during an intimate moment. Some women, once they are turned on, like to be, forgive the expression, manhandled. Many of us like both, depending on the moment and our mood. Communication is key here. You have to know what she is in the mood for. Don't worry. If you progress slowly, she will respond and let you know what she wants. All you have to do is pay attention.)

Some women need to be encouraged to become freer and less inhibited to feel sexier. Passionate kissing, with a little teasing, tends to bring the animal out in all of us. Tease her with your tongue, encourage her to reach out to you, pull back a little while kissing, and let her come to you. This will make her feel in control and sexually powerful. That's what you want! You want her to want you. (At this point, she should be reaching to remove your shirt, and her own. Let her signal when to disrobe. Again, it makes her feel in control and sexually powerful.)

- **Don't forget to set the mood.** Lock your bedroom door if you have kids! Play some sexy music and pull her close in a sensual dance. The closeness of your bodies will help increase the temperature between you, and the electricity too!

- **Don't forget to remind her of how much you love her while you are reinventing the art of kissing.** Telling your woman you love her, while you are showing her in a tender and romantic way, will score big bonus points for your Romance Account.

- **Kiss her eyelids, her throat, and behind her ears while you whisper how much you love her.** Don't forget to call her by name. Nothing melts a woman's heart like hearing her name whispered in her ear as you shower her with kisses, and mention all the other things you might like to do to her!

Now is the time to revisit that moment when all you wanted was to know her, to discover every single little thing that turned her on, to inhale every scent, every taste that makes her unique. Here is the difference: now you are older and wiser. You have learned a few tricks since you were so young and eager. Here is what you now know. Women are amazing creatures; they are soft, warm, and full of fire, but their fire must be released. Like a volcano, there needs to be a lot of shifting and encouragement under the surface for there to be a full eruption. To cause that eruption, you must be dedicated, patient, and gentle. Even though you may be unbelievably excited and ready to burst yourself, you have learned a huge lesson: your woman must come first. Why? Because she is potentially **MULTIORGASMIC**, even if she has not had the opportunity to experience it **yet**. Never, never, never forget that. Women are like the ocean, building up a wave, and then crashing on shore, then building up another wave and crashing upon the shore, over and over again. Your goal now, as a new man and her Love Warrior, is to help her discover that she is multiorgasmic. The best way to do that is to put her needs above your own and let her come to you. What this results in is that she will become so hot as she comes again and again that she will want you again and again, and your lovemaking will result in higher highs for her. Every orgasm takes her to the next level. She will be in a state of ecstasy that she may have never known until now all because of you. Now that she is reaching out to you, pulling you closer for deeper kisses, and running her fingers through your hair, it is time to expand to the next step.

CHAPTER II.
The Value of Sensual Touch—Connecting Through Massage

We have already talked about how important it is to re-establish a level of touch in your relationship, especially if you have been distant lately. One of the most popular complaints we get from couples all over the world, in a variety of age ranges, is that neither partner is satisfied. The picture is usually the same: she wants more affection and he wants more sex. By now, we are confident that you have learned a few things and can solve this situation on your own. The steps to rebuilding the bridge back to each other are small and simple, starting with improving your communication, breaking the touch barrier in small, daily ways like holding hands, cuddling, and kissing, and spending more time together. So maybe now she feels like she is consistently getting more affection, but she may not be ready to have sex more often. Why not?

A lost art in many relationships is the art of touch. For women, touch has to come after all the things we've talked about so far, because, otherwise, when you reach out to touch her in a sensual way, she's going to think you only want one thing: sex. Well, what's wrong with that? There's nothing wrong with wanting sex, but if you go about asking for it in the wrong way, or assume just because you're married that you don't need to woo her anymore to get lucky, you won't get any. Don't take our word for it—look at your own relationship and tell us this—if she doesn't feel close to you, if she doesn't feel loved by you, do you get any? Didn't think so. How about when she feels loved, or on the occasion that you make her feel sexy by noticing a new haircut or a new dress (or how much better an old one fits now that she's been exercising more)? We'll bet that now she may be humming a different tune when you slip your arms around her waist.

So how do you progress from holding hands and flirtatious kissing to sensual touch? Massage is an amazing way for couples to reconnect physically while opening the door for a sexual reconnection. This is especially important for couples that may be disconnected from each other on a physical level. Remember, we are tactile creatures; we need touch to survive and thrive. Many of us become disconnected from our own bodies due to illness, disfigurement, or weight gain. There are so many reasons: pregnancy and childbirth, menopause, erectile dysfunction, cancer, etc. The challenge in any relationship is to overcome these issues and bond again in a new way. The most important level to reconnect on is the physical level. The easiest way to do that, and the least intimidating, is body massage.

We are not suggesting that you need to run out and get your massage certification. What you might want to do is look for pleasant-smelling massage oil or a rich skin cream and start to touch each other again. You will want to start with shoulders and back, or hands and feet, so the act of massage isn't perceived as too sexual. It's OK if a massage is just a massage. If you begin to like it, or if you're terrified to start, pick up a book on massage and educate yourself on a few basic techniques. Massage also has another incredible benefit: it reduces stress almost immediately. Nothing makes being in the mood more possible than reducing stress.

Massage techniques hold some intriguing secrets too. Did you know that there are reflexology points in the feet that correspond to over thirty different parts of the body? Massaging poor, tired, aching feet can revitalize not only your spirit but different organs, glands, and internal systems as well. The benefits of rubbing these points can be numerous, including calmness and serenity, improved circulation, increased energy, and balanced emotions among many others. A foot massage will leave your lover's feet fresh, attractive, and tingling, and she will feel better all over.

One of the gentlest ways to introduce more touch into your relationship is offer to rub your lover's feet while sitting in front of the television at night. There isn't anything terribly sexual about it. All it says is that you noticed she's probably beat and might enjoy a little relief. But what it also says is that you are a sensual guy, and she feels that this is a big step in physical affection, one where sex isn't expected. A foot massage is a special thing to do for someone you love, and it deserves a special cream for the occasion. We have a few favorites: **Intimate Organics**, the certified organic line of products we carry on our store site, makes three fabulous **Foot ForePlay Lotions** in different scents that have different properties to relax her, to energize her, or to seduce her! Try them. Their viscosity and deep emollients are amazing for the rough, dry skin of the feet, and the scents are not girly, so you can use them too! The creams are also rich, which helps prevent your hands from getting tired too quickly, which is a common complaint. It works great on hands too, especially if she works on a computer all day.

Esther: One of the fastest and easiest ways to win HUGE bonus points with your better half is to offer to give her a massage, even if it's just a particular body part. Nothing turns me on more than when Joni offers me an unsolicited foot massage after a long day on my feet in high heels. She is instantly my savior...and my fantasy!

Love Her Right

So what if she really likes your foot rubs...what's next? It's time to expand your repertoire. Try rubbing larger parts of the body. The best place to start is the back and shoulders, since it's the most common part of the body we hold stress in. First, try what comes naturally, and just begin to touch. Use a good massage oil or cream (it's a personal preference) that will make her back slippery and your hands slide so you can rub longer. (There are several great brands on our Web site. Intimate Organics and Kama Sutra are two of our favorites, and we love the BWarm candles that melt into an amazing massage oil!) Start with your whole hand, and be sure to communicate with her, because you want to be sure you are using the right pressure. Too much and you're crushing her, not enough and she won't feel much. Communicating is simple during massage; if she's moaning softly, that's a good thing! Just be sure it's pleasure, not pain. Massage can also be deep, using the thumbs to dig in behind and underneath the shoulder blades, where big balls of stress hide. If your hands start to get tired, and she's lying down, try using your forearms up her back in a half clockwise and half counterclockwise motion. This will take the pressure off your tired hands and extend the massage a little too. From here, learning some technique may come in handy. There are about a zillion books available on the basics of body massage, so hit your local bookstore or Amazon and do a little research. Remember, you're a Love Warrior now. Finding new ways to pleasure your lover is your responsibility and your calling!

One of the best ways to learn is to seek out a massage professional. There are many great massage therapists out there who will book you an informational couple session, either at their office or your home, where they will teach you how to massage each other based on what your individual bodies need. Find someone you both like, or at least someone she has had a massage from before, and ask if that person would be willing to set up this kind of a teaching session. There are also numerous resorts and spas that offer couples massages, where you can both share a room and have therapists working on you at the same time. Many of these places will offer to teach couples techniques for doing massage on each other at home.

For the more adventurous, or once you have rebuilt your bridge back to one another and are looking for something more, you may want to think about erotic massage. Different than just a plain old back rub, erotic massage is about a sensual and sexual experience. This is where the massage is designed, by the techniques you use, to encourage sex play and orgasm. There are several ways to learn about erotic massage, and all of them are fun! On our store site, you will find DVDs, books with many colorful pictures, and even a deck of erotic massage technique cards to inspire your imagination and creativity. Using massage as a seduction technique is tantalizing, and erotic massage takes your sex play up to the next level. Just be sure that you are both on the same page and ready for it!

Remember, the point here is about touch, so start soft and tender, with only her pleasure in mind. The beautiful thing about giving physical pleasure is that it nourishes you both in body, mind, and spirit. It also invites reciprocity, especially if you don't go into a massage expecting one in return. So, if she wants to massage you too, let her, even if you feel it's not manly. It will feel great and make you feel sexy. The best part about learning to give and receive massage is that you have rebuilt that physical connection that you were striving for without ever demanding sex. She will love you for it, and the door to more touch—sexual touch—will open on its own.

Love Her Right

Now it's time to talk about The Big Kahuna, where seduction leads to lovemaking. To truly captivate your woman, and become Love Warriors together, mastering the arts of seduction and foreplay techniques is mandatory to guarantee amazing sex for you both.

CHAPTER 12.
Set The Stage With Loving Seduction

One of the most wonderful ways to progress to an amazing sexual encounter is to plan a seduction. While this might sound like a cheesy soap opera scene, seductions on soaps are so popular because they work...on and off the set. One of our favorite ways of explaining how men and women differ sexually is from Taoist sexuality (an ancient branch of Chinese medicine). Women are like water ("yin" in Asian discussion); men are more like fire ("yang"). While we all have elements of fire and water in our personalities, for the purposes of seduction, you have to focus on the fact that women need to be brought to a boil—their arousal needs to be stoked by your fire energy. We understand that, for you, your fire has you raring to go from the mere mention of a sexual encounter—a wink during dinner, a soft caress while you're loading the dishwasher—all have the power to make you weak in the knees and strong in the groin. Women take longer to get their engines running. It starts in our minds and hearts.

By this point, you have hopefully been applying everything you have learned so far, and you've been making your life together a more passionate experience. Communicating better, understanding what you both need to feel loved, and spending more time together have brought you closer and have made your woman feel like you have been courting each other all over again. The next natural step is to rediscover each other sexually; hopefully, by now, you are both ready to progress to that level. Incorporate romance into your ventures across this bridge, and make your sexual experience one you will both remember and want to repeat as often as possible! Planning a seduction does more than entice a woman to your bed; it makes her feel romanced and emotionally connected, which makes her feel sexy and desirable.

To go from feeling sexy to wanting to have sex is a gentle and easy progression for women; it's getting her to this place mentally and emotionally that's the challenge. The easiest way to do that is with a seduction. Sex for women begins with their brains getting turned on.

We understand that men are not the biggest fans of chick flicks and soap operas, so we thought you might need help in the creativity department. Below you will find different scenarios for seductions that might turn you both on. Try them out, alter them for your needs, and then try to create your own. You may discover that there is quite the Don Juan inside of you; all you needed was a little inspiration to let him out! (And the best part: seduction planning is made easy at our Web site www. LoveHerRightStore.com. Everything you could possibly need, from rose petals to massage products, lingerie to candles, at one convenient location—all at prices that won't extinguish your fire!)

*Be sure to plan ahead. Don't execute your planned seduction on a day she already has eight hundred things to do. Clear her schedule by making a date with her first. You can still surprise her!

*If you have kids, arrange for them to be out for more than a couple of hours—you want to have time to truly seduce your beautiful woman, and you don't want to get caught in the middle of your romantic master plan—it's not a turn on!

(If you don't have child care available, check out our suggestion for creating a Couple Time Support Team with other parents in Chapter 4.)

Seduction #1

Set the scene so that when your partner comes home from the store, she finds a trail of flower petals that begins at the front door and leads to the bedroom. (Visit your local florist and tell them you need rose petals—they should have old roses that are not salable to give you cheap, or you can purchase silk scented rose petals that are reusable for your next seduction.) There, you will be waiting, wearing something sexy like a silk robe or boxers, with champagne on ice if your budget allows. Candles are lit, there's soft music playing in the background, and the bed is covered with rose petals. All that is missing is the two of you to roll around in them. Depending on your available cash, you can also have a little surprise for her...something sexy to wear that shows her how desirable she is.

Seduction #2

Tape a note to the front door, telling her to come inside and continue to look for clues; this is a treasure hunt! Have a trail of discarded clothing lead to your next clue, a note taped to the bathroom door (which is shut) telling her to drop her clothes, and that you will be in charge of picking them up! If she has a light robe, you can have it hanging on the doorknob, and ask her to put it on. Then, she is to open the door where she will find a plethora of candles and a steamy bubble bath waiting, two glasses (plastic, please!) of wine or a beverage of your choice, and maybe you are already in the tub, looking irresistible. Start by washing each other and let the caressing begin! (Just be sure to time this right if you are planning on waiting in the tub; you don't want to turn into a prune if she is late or have the water turn cold!)

🕯 Seduction #3

Lead her to the bedroom with a sprinkling of flower petals that begins at the front door. A note is taped to the closed door of your bedroom, which asks her to drop her clothes and put on a soft silk robe, a negligee, or a towel hanging on the knob. When she opens the door, she will find the room lit by candlelight, with soft music playing or maybe the sound of the ocean in the background, and you standing next to the bed with massage oil in hand. Ask her to lie on the bed face down and give her a romantic massage to rub away all the stress of her day. (Our favorite products for this seduction are BWarm Candles. They have beautiful scents that are not girly or overly floral, and as the candle melts, it turns into a warm, luxurious massage oil. Just blow out the candle first and count to twenty before pouring it on her skin. You don't want any discomfort! This oil is some of the greatest stuff we have ever tried. The viscosity makes it easy to slip and slide. For some reason, you will find that your hands won't get as tired as they usually do with no oil or when using other products. Try them, and let us know if you agree!) You can also use baby oil, olive oil, or skin cream as inexpensive alternatives.

🕯 Seduction #4

Remember when she asked you to take a cooking class and you grudgingly agreed? Well, now you get to strut your stuff. Plan a seduction that includes making her a romantic dinner. This means going the whole nine yards: picking what recipes you want to use, doing the shopping, preparing the meal, setting the table (use good dishes and real silverware for this special occasion!) and don't forget the candles, music, and possibly flowers. You have creative options with this seduction; you can make a series of finger foods to feed each other as a picnic in front of the fire, or in bed, you can make a truly fancy meal if you are at home in the kitchen, with a gooey yummy dessert that can be eaten off each other's bodies in the bedroom. Refer to the aphrodisiac chapter for food suggestions and menus!

🦋 Seduction #5

Plan a game night. As we have discussed, communication is key when reestablishing a passionate sexual relationship. One of the best ways we have found to do that in a nonthreatening way is to play games. The concept is the same, but the rewards—oh, baby! Communication is key with these games because they allow you to explore what turns you both on physically and emotionally. On our store Web site, we feature a great selection of board games for adults that can help remove barriers to communication and allow you to speak freely, and touch freely, while enjoying each other in sensual and romantic ways. Some games, like Synchrohearts, are about romance and communication, with some sexy fun thrown in. Others, like Discover Your Lover or 101 Nights of Grrrreat Sex, are all about true seduction. Respect where your relationship is today and pick what kind of game would work for you. Be sure to have all the tools you may need: massage oil, something sexy and easy to remove to wear, candles, and soft music. You never know when a game may lead to something more serious…

Dr. Joni: If you are communicating fairly well, how about a game of strip poker? You might want to plan what you have hidden under the outer layer of clothing for an extra surprise!

Seduction #6

Every woman wants to feel beautiful. You can help her with that by planning a spa day at home or at the spa. Start by making her breakfast in bed—and have one red rose with a little bud vase for the tray. (Even the most hopeless cook can handle breakfast—keep it simple; it's the thought that counts.) After breakfast, ask her to shower and tell her you have a surprise for her when she's done. Then, the choice is yours: if you want to do it yourself, have her join you in the bedroom, propped up on pillows, and sipping a glass of juice from a wine glass while you begin to rub her feet. Then, you will use a pumice stone or any other kind of tool to remove the dead skin from her tired tootsies and make her feet smooth and silky. Apply a little more cream now and rub her feet again, and up her calves. Here's the fun part: pull out a sexy nail polish, like a fire engine red, and paint her toenails. Don't worry if you're not good at it; she will be charmed by how romantic you are, and all this pampering will make her feel sexy.

If this terrifies you, and finances allow, try delegating. After her shower, take her to a local spa for a day of pampering. If you're into it, you can plan a couple's massage, where you will share a room while simultaneously receiving a professional massage. Depending on your time and finances, you can really go for it and arrange for her to have a facial or a manicure and pedicure too. We'll bet there are some cool treatments for you too, no matter how manly you are. There is nothing feminine or sissy like about soft skin, especially if that grizzly face is planning on being in sensitive skin territory anytime soon! After your day of beauty, try a light lunch and one of the most decadent of pleasures—afternoon delight! Don't save afternoon sex just for vacations; there is something truly delicious about it!

Dr. Joni: Many towns have massage and spa treatment schools that provide services for greatly reduced fees. The students get to practice, and you get to save money while your honey gets pampered. It's a great deal for everyone!

🐟 Seduction #7

If your budget allows, take your woman out to a fabulous restaurant for a romantic dinner. Get all dressed up and tell her you want to show her off, so either pick out the dress you want her to wear or ask her to get something new and sexy. Do you dance? How about a hot new club where you can dance the night away? What she doesn't know is that after dinner and dancing, you and she will be spending a romantic evening away from home in a luxurious hotel suite for the night. You will have to make all of the necessary arrangements, including child care, reservations, and packing an overnight bag for the two of you. Be sure to include all of your tricks of the trade: massage oil, candles, music, rose petals for the bed, toys, and anything else you might need for a night of sexual exploration. No one is going to bother you, there are no phones, e-mails, pagers, or kids to interrupt you tonight, so be prepared to have a night to remember! Order a bottle of champagne to be delivered to the room and left on ice for your arrival after dinner. Be sure to not eat too heavy—you don't want to spend the evening nursing a sour stomach instead of making mad, passionate love!

Finances and child care permitting, this can be a lot of fun, and it's a great seduction idea for a special occasion like a birthday or anniversary, especially if you need to rationalize the expense. You can even get the kids in on the secret, which will help make sure that they don't freak out that you'll be gone for the night. Just be sure they won't spill the beans!

The only limits to the concept of seduction are your own creativity and imagination. You are also surrounded by inspiration: watch your woman and discover what turns her on. When you watch movies together, does she respond to certain love scenes? Do specific things turn her on, like flowers, music, or massage? Begin to gather this information by being a more observant partner. With all of this ammunition, plus all of the great information she has already given you from the Language of Love chapter's exercise, you will have all of the hints you need to plan the perfect seductions for her. Remember, maintain a sense of adventure and a sense of humor. Not every seduction may work out as planned, and sometimes life gets in the way, but, for women, the gift is truly in the effort. She will be surprised and delighted by how much time and thought you put into planning and executing a seduction, and that alone will transform the way she sees you. She will feel romanced, loved, and cherished, which makes her feel sexy. Besides, how can she resist such a romantic?

Well, the time has come to get down to the details you have been waiting for. What can we show you and teach you about lovemaking that can transform your love life and revitalize your relationship? Let's find out.

CHAPTER 13.
Hand Play That Will Make Her Scream!

If you, as a lover, are capable of using your mouth and hands with expertise on a woman, she will be begging you for more. Most women surveyed revealed that their favorite sex acts are manual and oral pleasuring and are the preferred methods for her to orgasm. No, the size of your penis doesn't matter, although the width seems to be a benefit, but we'll address that later. Women are like a new car engine that needs to be warmed up before you take her for the big ride, so let's cover the basics first and then more advanced information about hand and manual play.

First: Do we have to remind you to wash your hands? Clean hands are an absolute must because "stuff" under your fingernails can stay there *for thirty days*. Yes, we said 30 days! Buy a nail brush and learn how to use it, especially under the fingernails. Your woman will appreciate not getting vaginal infections from whatever you had your hands in for the last month! Make sure that your fingernails are short and smooth, and use moisturizer on your hands daily after work to keep you hands Love Warrior ready!

Ok, back to business…We'll assume that you have been touching and kissing and are both interested in going to the next step. Do not shortcut the kissing stage because women love to be kissed during foreplay, intercourse, and afterplay. Soon, you are going to start to touch her with your hands, and she might start to touch you too!

It is now time to let your hands and lips wander. Take your kisses down the sides and middle of her throat, and run your hands down the side of her body. Using your fingertips in a soft motion, glide gently over her skin, all the way down to her waist. As you kiss her neck, if she is responsive, she should be tilting her head back to offer you her throat—this is an excellent sign. As your hands come back up the side of her body, use your palms and fingertips and the back of your hands to stroke her. This variety of touch stimulates the skin, which is by far the biggest erogenous zone of the human body. Using a very gentle touch (but not tickling her), let your hands wander all over her skin, up and down her arms, over her breasts, back up along her back, and into her hair, all the while kissing her mouth like this is the first time you have ever seen her topless. (If you haven't taken clothes off yet, slip her top off now, as long as she is willing. Chances are she has pulled it off herself by now.)

Move your kisses down to the beautiful crease between her breasts, and gently brush your fingers over a breast. Cup her breast in your hand, and use your palm to gently stimulate the nipple. It should harden (stand up at attention) at your touch. If not, then you can GENTLY apply just a slight pressure, squeezing the nipple between your thumb and finger if she is not too sensitive. While cupping her breast, begin kissing this breast with gentle, soft kisses. Use your tongue to softly lick her nipple. Sometimes using the middle part of your tongue, where your tongue is soft and flat, over her nipple gives a more consistent pressure than the tip, especially if her breasts are sensitive. Now, place your entire mouth over her breast, or as much of it as you can if she is large breasted, and gently inhale through your mouth, causing a gentle suckling motion. Run your tongue around the breast in your mouth, and pull back a little so that you are now using your mouth to play with her nipple. Don't focus on suckling too much. If you have children, this might be too familiar for her...not in a sexy way. Check in with her to make sure she's as turned on as you are! Move to the opposite breast and play with that one too—can't play favorites you know!

Dr Joni: Be sure that you are communicating the whole time. If she begins to pull away while you are in the middle of breast play, it may mean that her breasts are too sensitive for aggressive fondling. That's why gentle touch is so important. Remember, during certain points in her menstrual cycle her breasts may be so sensitive that any touch is painful, not pleasurable. She may also be pushing her torso forward, putting more of her breast in your mouth, giving you the signal that she is enjoying your touch and that you can be more aggressive with your hands or mouth. You have to get used to watching for her signals; this is what sets an amazing lover apart from the rest.

Now begin to move down her body, sliding down lower against her, taking your kisses down with you. With luck, clothes are strewn all over the floor by now, and you are both nude, or close to it. Kiss her along her belly, and begin stroking her along the sides of her body and up and down her legs, including the back of her thighs and behind her knees. You can begin to gently stroke up and down her inner thighs with a soft touch—fingertips or palms only. You can also kiss the insides of her thighs, but no other oral play yet. Glide those fingertips only temptingly over her genital area—just tease her for now. If she is still wearing any undergarments, tease her through the fabric at first, and then slip them off as your touch glides along her outer thighs. Remember, the skin is so sensitive right now that every touch is sending messages of pleasure to her brain, and you can tell by how her body moves. As she begins to moan and writhe on the bed, or slither closer to you, these are all the signs you need that you are doing something right. Be sure to pay close attention and watch. Look for signs of her coming to you. If you're not sure, ask her if it feels good!

OK, remember the section where we talked about female anatomy? Yeah, we know you may have thought that part would be a little boring, but you have to know what you are playing with. Here is where it comes in handy. (If you skipped over that chapter or don't really remember it, go back and review it now. The information is vital if you want these techniques to work!)

Slide down her body so that you can look at her genitalia. Tell her how beautiful she is. You should see her outer and inner lips, how one lip is larger than the other, and that they may be a little puffy due to arousal. At top dead center, or thereabouts, you should be able to see the hood of the clitoris. This whole area is incredibly sensitive (remember, over 8,000 nerve endings are located in the clitoris alone). Because of this, some women may not enjoy direct clitoral stimulation, especially before they are fully aroused. Start by using the palm of your hand and gently start to trace circles over her pubic hair. Play with the curls of hair with your fingers and apply a little pressure with your palm over her clitoris. This way, you won't be touching her sensitive zones until they are ready. You will feel her clitoral shaft and clitoris harden under your touch as she gets turned on. Even when a woman masturbates, each woman's needs are different, so go slowly, watch her, and ask her to tell you what feels good to her, or for her to show you. Watching can be quite the turn-on!

One of the great features of using hand play to bring your woman to orgasm is its versatility. You can be face-to-face, staring into each other's eyes, deep in passionate kisses, or whispering erotic little secrets in her ear while stroking her. Once you are familiar with the terrain and have a sense of where she likes to be touched, glide back up her body so you can enjoy the connection of these techniques.

Place your hand palm side down over her genital mound, fingers pointing toward her toes. **VERY GENTLY** place two or three fingertips together, around the clitoral area, but not directly on the clitoris, focusing on the area on her pubic bone, and softly stimulate her. Start at the top of her pubic area and use your fingers on the sides of her clitoral shaft and trace all the way down to near the opening of her vagina. Don't enter her yet. Watch her body and her reactions to your touch. If she wants you to apply greater pressure, she will move toward you, pushing her hips forward; or, if you are lucky, she will just tell you! You will probably feel and maybe even see that she is wet, and the key here is to stay consistent. When she starts to get wet, you will notice how direct she likes the pressure, whether closer or farther away from direct contact with the clitoris. Every woman is different, so you need to communicate about what turns her on the most. (Be aware that many women have never had the ability to verbally tell a man about their sexual needs during sex before, so she may be shy about telling you exactly what the best touch is for her. Discover it together.) Remember, with stimulating the clitoris, whether directly or indirectly, consistency is key. You must strike a rhythm, moving with the gyrating of her hips, and keep the pressure and speed the same. You will be able to tell if she wants you to vary, but, once she's approaching orgasm, do not vary the tempo unless she tells you to. It's like a slow dance—you don't just switch over to a salsa in the middle of a waltz.

Every woman likes a different style of clitoral stimulation finger work, so let's go over a few typical options that women use when masturbating so you can have a little insider information on how to be a Master Love Warrior using your hands. Start by using your fingers (two or three) in a figure eight movement, brushing over her clitoris with the pads of your fingers, making the figure eights smaller and smaller until you are starting to focus on the clitoris and clitoral shaft; this will get her juices flowing without directly touching her clitoral head.

Next, spread your fingers apart and put one finger on each side of her clitoral shaft. Rub gently back and forth, up and down the length of her clitoral shaft. This is a mini version of the hand job that she gives you! If you need a little lube, use it, or a little saliva, or touch between her vaginal labia to see if she is getting wet and use her juices to slide over her more easily. The better she is able to get wet, the more fun she will have as you vary the pressure and speed as you stroke her to climax.

Now try taking your first and second fingertip pads and rub over the clitoris hood in small, gentle circles, varying the pressure and speed until she is moving with you and guiding you. Some women enjoy a side-to-side motion. As you use this, you may try to start to increase the speed of the side-to-side motion on her clitoris. If you slide your fingers toward her vaginal opening, keep up the side-to-side motion with the part of your fingers nearest to your palm and use your fingertips to touch the opening of her vagina and tease her labia and perineum. You might even tease her by inserting a little bit of your fingertip into her, to see her reaction!

As the tension builds up inside of her, all of her is very sensitive, and you may want to use your other hand to pull her closer, just to let her know that you are cradling her while she gets ready to come. Don't vary your speed; just let her come to you. Patience is a virtue here, so don't be in a hurry. This may take some practice, because it can be hard to control yourself when she's getting so turned on. Unless you're made of stone, by now, you're pretty hot too, because watching her come is very sexy. Some women take a long time; some can come over and over again in the span of minutes. Take in the sights while you watch her: her scent, how she looks, watch her face. Kiss her breasts and neck to give her multiple areas of stimulation in order to turn her on. She will tell you when to go to the next step. You Go, Lover Boy!

Penetration—Fingers Style

When you insert your fingers into her, there are some fabulous places to touch inside her to drive her wild. The most commonly talked about is the G-Spot. Named after Dr. Ernst Grafenberg, it is located inside of her vagina about 1 ½ to 2 inches in, just beyond the hard pubic bone, on the upper pelvic wall. As you curl your finger up to massage this spongy area that's only about the size of a dime or a quarter, it will swell and harden with gentle massage. There are some fabulous G-Spot stimulating gels available. Our favorite is by Intimate Organics called the Discover G-Spot Stimulating Gel. If you need help with the hand and finger positions, please refer to the anatomy section where we have photos to guide you into the right place. Here are several additional areas to stimulate that we discovered in our curiosity about other sexual techniques. The Taoists 3000 years ago were among the first sexologists and were a branch of Chinese medicine. They were physicians who specialized in sexual play as a form of physical healing. This is how we discovered the X and Y spots. They are located to the left and right side of the G-Spot area of your partner's vagina. They are also located in the first third of the vaginal opening like the G-Spot. Using your fingers to circle around this band of muscles will stimulate these areas as well. You may try using two fingers to start and adding fingers as your partner needs to fill her enough to get the level of pleasure that she might want or need at each encounter.

Love Her Right

It is most common for men to use their fingers together, like a penis, and thrust in and out, but there are more interesting variations to try. Try using your fingers in a scissor-like action inside her vagina (one finger is up, while the other is down.) This gives her pleasure on the front and back wall of the vagina at the same time. Vary the depth of penetration with your fingers and pay attention to her body language. Also, vary the speed, slow down and then arouse her with faster thrusts to keep her from getting bored. Try using several fingers together, tracing in figure eight motions inside her to touch her G-spot, X and Y spots alternately.

Please try not to jam your fingers inside her too hard, unless she likes it a little rougher and deeper. Many women can handle having your entire hand inside of her for pleasure, especially after childbirth, when the walls of the vagina have stretched and she needs the width of the penetration for her ultimate pleasure.

When looking for a rhythm to give some consistency to your lovemaking, might we suggest using the beat of some sexy music in the background? That way, you will know that you have a tempo to keep to, and you can focus on keeping the pressure consistent. Music can be a wonderful guide...give it a try!

Esther: To completely add to her experience, use your mouth to kiss hers, or use your mouth on her clitoris while fingering her. If she enjoys oral sex, we highly recommend offering to help her climax by using your mouth on her clitoris while you use your hands inside of her.

So, you might be asking us, "How do I use my mouth and hands at the same time?" Trust us, it's easy and worth it; just settle into a good position for your neck and have some fun. According to the Taoists, oral sex completes an energy circuit for higher sexual arousal, and you may even get a sexual jolt of energy from her as she climaxes in your mouth! For everything you need to know about oral sex, here come a few more of our lesbian secrets...

CHAPTER 14.
Our Best-Kept Secret: The Art Of Performing Oral Sex

Some women can climax, and quickly, from oral stimulation and some women cannot. The first time you follow this guide, she will probably come just from the sheer newness of it all. In fact, the majority of women surveyed revealed that oral stimulation was their preferred method of achieving orgasm. In a perfect world, she would climax once from your touch, or get so turned on that she would be begging you for your mouth to bring her to climax.

For a woman, the act of having oral sex performed on her can be viewed by two completely opposite views… one great and one not so great. Some women feel shame about their genitals, how they look, how they taste, and are they doing something "dirty." Thank goodness time has evolved, and both men and women have accepted the art of cunnilingus as a natural part of foreplay. Sometimes it may be the only form of sexual play depending on what kind of mood you're in. Many women have also realized that the intensity of their orgasm from receiving oral sex and the love and connection between the partners is highly erotic and desirable.

Dr. Joni: Needless to say, oral sex is a lesbian's favorite activity: both receiving and performing. Most straight women that we have spoken to LOVE receiving oral sex, and they say it makes them feel more passionate and bonded to their partner. Never forget that this is a very intimate act. We are here to guide you with our favorite techniques!

Again, communication and the drive that you have to be her Love Warrior will help her to get past any body issues that she may have since you are already lavishing her with compliments about how sexy she is and how fabulous she tastes! Some women take longer to orgasm than others, and it may vary due to hormones, stress, and her being self-conscious about her body. Some women have clitorises that are larger than other women's and may have larger labia, or one even larger than the other depending on individual anatomy. So what? Enjoy her for what she has been given and unlock the horny vixen that you crave. We feel that women that receive more oral sex may be more likely to give you oral sex too! That is the key to being intimate sexual partners.

Since most people are not taught tongue techniques, we are going to present several methods that have been described as favorites from women all over the world. Oral sex has been used as an erotic and orgasmic means for thousands of years, as early as 300 BC and was explicitly drawn on ceramic art pieces in India and China. Oral sex can be used alone, combined with *fellatio* or manual play. Both partners are involved, which heightens the intimacy and eroticism of the act. In many cultures, a man performing oral sex on his partner is believed to be able to connect his sexual energy with hers and gain sexual stamina and strength while giving her pleasure.

So, let's get down (or go down) and describe the techniques and responses that you can expect while making oral love to your partner. If you feel the need, please refer to the anatomy section—chapter 8 of this book to see the pictures of an exposed woman's genitalia (without hair) in order to clarify the most important parts of the female that we are going to refer to frequently.

So, you are between her legs, looking at her most intimate parts, her velvet oasis. She is aroused and maybe a little anxious, especially if this is new for both of you. Take time to just look at the natural beauty of her vagina and labia. Can you see her clitoris or is it hidden by a hood of skin? Her inner and outer labia have been aroused and are starting to become swollen with the touching from your hands, and she may be glistening with wetness from her excitement. Keep kissing her on her thighs and touching her, massaging her vulva, so that she does not feel like she is at the gynecologist but rather she is with her intimate erotic partner. She may be a little shy if you have not been orally sexual together until now. Make sure that she is relaxed and ready to receive one of the highest forms of sexual pleasure that she can dream of.

Take both hands and gently spread her lips (labia) apart. The secret here is that there are about a million different ways to stimulate her orally. The main point of your focus is on her clitoris. It has about 8000 nerve endings, which makes it a very powerful erotic spot. It has to be approached gently at first, before it will be able to be aroused enough for climax. Every stroke you can think of, from drawing your name with your tongue, spelling out the alphabet, counting by drawing numbers with your tongue and seeing how many numbers it takes to achieve orgasm…the list is endless.

If you experimented with your fingers as we recommended in the previous chapter, you know one place where she likes to be touched, so you can begin by using your tongue on that spot. At first, use only the middle of your tongue gently, to tease her just a little. Remember, every woman has a different level of sensitivity, and having the clitoris stimulated by your tongue instead of your fingers is something different entirely. Again, some women are very sensitive, so direct clitoral stimulation may be too much, so you need to experiment a little. Float your tongue around the entire area, from clitoral hood down to the perineum (that space between her vagina and her anus), which is very sensitive and a huge turn-on. Use your lips to tug and pull gently on her swollen labia. Kiss the area where her legs and her vulva connect. Blow soft air breaths on her pubic hair, not inside of her—ever. As she responds to your tongue, begin to use your tongue to touch softly and gently around her clitoral area, moving in a gentle up-and-down or side-to-side motion, like you're licking a lollypop or a dripping ice cream cone. With your tongue being soft and broad, you have the ability to cover more circumference of the clitoral hood, and apply more even pressure without pushing too hard directly. (Many women don't like the tip of the tongue, especially at first touch, for a host of reasons, not the least of which is that it can feel like you are being prodded with a hot poker. By using the middle of your tongue, it feels more like a warm, wet, encompassing feeling, which is a more consistent turn-on.)

Use your mouth now too, the way you did when playing with her breasts. Keep your lips over your teeth so that if you rest your face on her for balance she will not feel your teeth, which hurt and are incredibly distracting for her. We suggest that you use your neck strength to not rest the weight of your head on her at all so that she can concentrate on the sensations that you are giving her with your mouth and tongue. Gently inhale through your mouth, pulling her whole pubic area into your eager mouth. Suck gently on her clitoral hood, or glans, and you will feel that it has grown, much like a hardening penis. This gentle tugging is like when she is giving you a blow job.

Our Best-Kept Secret: The Art Of Performing Oral Sex

Be very attentive while you do this; some women don't like too much pressure, and the sucking feeling can be overwhelming. She will let you know if she pulls back or pushes you away a little to decrease the pressure. Just go steadily with the center of your tongue, and increase the pressure if she begins to ask for it by moving forward deeper into your mouth. Try putting the tip of your tongue inside her vagina periodically to tease her, too! Place little licks on her perineum to increase the anticipation and multiply her sensations. How long it takes her to come is as individual as her fingerprint. Be patient.

Don't change anything unless she asks you to. When she comes, you will know! The tension will build up, and her hips will begin to move more aggressively, and she *should* become vocal. Her wetness will increase, and her vaginal opening should widen in anticipation of more sexual stimulation inside her vagina. She may begin to grab the sheets, and you may want to slide your arms under her thighs and rock her hips closer toward you. Not only do you get a better angle, but you can cradle her while allowing her to reach down and grab your hand before or during her orgasm. You may feel the contractions inside her vagina while she comes. She may be begging you to insert some fingers into her to help her climax or to simultaneously stimulate her G-Spot.

If you are able to, stroke a breast while you are making love to her with your mouth; it will make her feel totally encompassed by your love! Softly stroke around her nipples, and every now and then give a slight tug or apply a little pressure to her nipples if it turns her on. Whisper sexy words to her about how hot she is, how wet she is getting, and how delicious she tastes! She may even run her fingers through your hair and grab it—don't be alarmed; that's a good thing! When she climaxes, it will feel like fireworks just went off inside of her, and her whole body will be teeming with little nerve ending firings, from her hair to her toenails. And you will be the Romeo of her dreams! She may even cry a little from the power of the release. Don't freak out! Just hold her, smile at her, and tell her how amazing she is!

Esther: No matter how evolved and sexually liberated your woman might be, we all have a lurking concern about the first time our partner goes down on us. Will my partner like the way I smell and taste? What if he or she doesn't? What if he or she is really grossed out? Reassurance takes a moment, but the results will be incredible. If your partner knows you like to go down on her almost as much as she likes having you there, you will be delighted at how often she invites you for a repeat performance!

Other tips and mouth techniques to try:

- Alternate circles with licks
- Lick her clitoris, dip into her vagina, then lick her clitoris again
- Alternate small circles on the sides of her clitoral hood
- Lick her clitoris side to side or up and down, then gently nibble or tug on her clitoris
- While licking her, use your thumb to apply pressure to the base of her clitoral shaft and gently roll it around under your finger
- Look straight into her eyes as you pleasure her and smile with joy that you are giving her passionate, intimate pleasure
- Trace the letters of the alphabet, spell her name with your tongue and get her so worked up that she can't help but to explode into your mouth!

- If you need to rest your neck, place your hand over her mons at the base of her clitoral shaft and rest your nose on the back of your hand while you use your tongue
- Keep your rhythm steady...vary the pressure with gently increasing intensity, but let her give you the verbal clues to get her to orgasm.

When a woman climaxes, her face becomes flushed, and her toes may even curl up. She may be panting and sweating, but needing more sexually. Sometimes a woman screams, calls out your name, evokes God's name, or she may be bucking or grinding into your face, but don't let her throw you off! After orgasm, she may push you off her and need to relax; you will understand her body language as you try more and more techniques.

Don't think that you are finished yet...she has the potential to be multiorgasmic, and this may be only the beginning of the most fun part of making love with your partner. What can you do to get her so turned on that she wants more from you? We like to view this as if she is your new toy...what can you try in order to make sure that she is so satisfied sexually that you will never have to worry about her turning you down? Just think about all of the fun, sexual acts that you can experiment with when you have two willing and able partners!

She may want you to combine oral sex with manual stimulation or with penetration. Obviously, you can't put your penis inside of her while you are happily going down on her, but you could use a vibrator, dildo, or clitoral stimulator. Or, she may choose to masturbate while you add in a little licking and tonguing her and maybe use some toy play while you watch. Or, she may want to perform *fellatio* on you at the same time (69), as she wants to return the favor, knowing that you are good and hard by now! Think about all of the creative combinations that you can try before you have even thought about intercourse!

Esther: When she loses count, you have done your job and achieved Love Warrior status! Welcome to the club!

Remember that the techniques that may have worked for you with prior partners may not work with your present partner. In fact, her needs may change from day to day and month to month, depending on her hormonal swings. Don't be put off or take it personally! Just ask her, "How may I please you? Do you want me to go softer, harder, slower, faster, etc..." Ask her to show you where to touch her. Does she like it when you use your tongue in circles? Does suction feel good? How about top to bottom or long strokes? Suggest that she use her words while you perform oral sex on her to guide you. It is not criticism when she is giving you guidance...you just can't feel her sensations, and the guidance will leave you both feeling satisfied! That is the true Love Warrior: a lover who is so interested in making her feel good that you care enough to ask her how to satisfy her in the way that **she** needs.

Have you been squeamish about performing oral sex on her? Is it a concern about her taste? Remember, every woman is different, and the taste and smell of her vaginal fluids can change based on her diet, medications she is taking, and where she is in her menstrual cycle. Although most of these are normal for her, it may make oral sex less enjoyable for the performer. You may consider the easiest answer, which is to perform sex in the shower or just after showering together. Another option is the use of a dental dam or plastic wrap, especially if she has a medical history of an STD (sexually transmitted disease). These include genital herpes, and HIV. Never perform oral sex after using a condom with the spermicidal cream nonoxynol-9...it tastes awful! Have oral sex first, then proceed to intercourse.

Also, be aware that the foods that we eat can change the flavor of women's natural love juices. Kiwi, celery, and pineapple make her taste sweeter, so you might want to create a love dessert before the sex play begins!

What about her—is she squeamish about receiving oral sex? This is more common than you may think, and very disheartening for both you and us. Oral sex is an incredible source of pleasure for both men and women, and it saddens us to think that some people would limit their sexual pleasure for any reason by choice. However, if women have been sexually abused or have serious body issues, they may not be comfortable with this sex act. It is going to take a good deal of communication and some work on your part to let her know that you really enjoy giving her pleasure and that you are willing to experiment. This is the same kind of communication and work that it will take if she does not enjoy performing oral sex on you, and you would like to change that. (If she does not enjoy performing oral sex on you, try using a flavored condom.) Expanding your sexual repertoire is a two-way street, and we believe in the give-to-get concept. If you want to receive more oral sex play, you have to start by giving more oral sex play, no way around that. If either of you has a flat-out no-way policy on the subject—OK—move on and try something else. Making sure you are both sexually satisfied is the goal, no matter how you get there.

How about oral sex during menstruation? For some men, this may seem like something you would rather avoid, but every sexual encounter involves body fluids, yours and hers. Menstrual blood comes from her vagina, and it does not affect her clitoris or other external sex organs. An easy way to avoid the fluids associated with her period and still have oral sex is to wash up first and insert a tampon. If she doesn't use tampons and won't put one in just for oral sex, then you might want to wait until her flow is diminished or gone. You can also replace oral play with hand play if this just doesn't work for you. Remember that women are incredibly aroused during their periods, due to her increased hormone levels, so she may really love receiving any and every form of sexual pleasure during this time. And since she's so turned on, chances are she will want to return the oral favor!

Esther: Some men just can't wrap their heads around the concept of performing oral sex during their partner's period. We have experience here—in a lesbian relationship, you have two women getting their periods, and not always at the same time, so if you think that we're not going to be sexual for two weeks out of the month, guess again! That's the second best reason that tampons were invented!

Plan a seduction...start foreplay or massage, then touching sensually, then sexually. Nothing works better than to engage as many senses as you can and to stimulate as many places, mentally and physically, to transform you both into insatiable sexual partners! Not feeling creative? Refer back to our seduction chapter for some suggestions! Just don't let anything stand in the way of recreating your sex life!

We know that by now you are hot and looking forward to intercourse. It's time to take a walk on the wild side and spice up those familiar positions or maybe try something new....

CHAPTER 15.
Who's On Top: Trying New Positions For Intercourse

So many positions to try to keep your sex hot!

There are hundreds of positions in which to engage in mind-blowing sexual intercourse. Some of them are more physically engaging than others, and some offer options to free up hands and mouths for fondling, stroking, and teasing your lover. Many have even been named to help describe them. Some are a little naughty, but feel great! We are going to offer several with slight, but interesting variations for pleasure for both of you! Variety is critical to keeping your sex life hot; trying different positions and asking your lover what feels good will keep you on the path to being our Master Love Warrior!

Man on Top

The most time-tested and frequently used position for intercourse is called the "missionary position." Most men love this position because they are in control. The man is on top, with the woman's legs spread around him. Although this is a classic position, it is not always the most interesting from an erotic or pleasure perspective, especially for the woman. Ah, why, you ask? First, most women are not able to climax in this position, since there is almost no clitoral stimulation. Also, the weight of a large man on top of a woman may literally take her breath away, and not in a good way. So, unless you guys are doing your push-ups and can hold up your body weight, your woman is getting crushed. A suggestion to avoid crushing her would be for the man to kneel while entering her, thus giving you deep penetration, and you can both breathe and moan!

©Akeim Ford

Now, if you want to add variety, try placing one or two pillows under her buttocks. This little addition will cause her to lift her pelvis, and you might be able to rub your penis against her G-Spot, which will give her more pleasure. But there are many more positions to try that don't require you to be an Olympic gymnast to achieve mutual sexual satisfaction and have many orgasms between you!

Also, try using shallower thrusting, since the first third of a woman's vagina is the most sensitive. Or tease her by alternating shallow and deeper thrusts. The shallow thrusts will pleasure you while giving her more pressure on her G-Spot (a VERY sensitive spot), and the deep thrusts will give YOU a chance to calm down and delay ejaculation. Take your time while teasing her with alternating in-and-out moves, figure 8 hip moves, and short or deep thrusts. This will give her a chance to get more arousal and crave the release of the orgasm. You may want to ask her to touch her clitoris at the same time you are inside of her... watching her pleasure herself may lead to mutual and multiple orgasms.

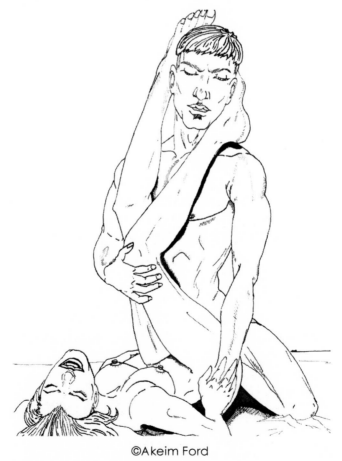

©Akeim Ford

Other variations on the missionary position usually involve changing where her legs are. For example, have her fold her legs up onto her chest and then you enter her from the front. She can wrap her arms around your back under your armpits and you get to penetrate her deeply. If she is flexible, she can straighten her legs to rest on your shoulders with her knees bent. You get to watch her face as you thrust into her, kissing her and holding each other all the while. Another leg option is to have the woman wrap her legs around your waist or hips like you are two vines entwined together. You have close and deep contact, and you can rock, roll, and thrust yourself into hot climaxes. More leg options are having the woman raise her feet up toward the ceiling, but with her legs together. You enter her vagina; if you are kneeling, it is like the doggy style position, but with her on her back.

Woman on Top

Try having your woman mount you with you on your back and with her facing you. Sometimes this is called the "cowgirl" position. This allows her to control the depth, speed, and pace of your penetration. She may be kneeling over you or lying up against you. If she kneels, you have the advantage of having your hands free to fondle her breasts or clitoris. She can also reach behind herself and play with your balls. Yahoo! You can add a clitoral vibrator or special lubes and vary the spots that are getting stimulated and how intense you want it at that particular moment. She can lean down for kissing and putting her breasts in your mouth too!

©Akeim Ford

You can also perform the cowgirl positions with the man in a sitting position. Everyone's hands are free, and you can touch each other everywhere and anywhere... so can she! You can sit with your legs crossed or straight.

©Akeim Ford

If you have the strength, you can push yourselves off the bed and bounce up to meet her as she pushes down on you. You get very deep penetration, and you can kiss or suck on her breasts, too. You or she can play with her clitoris while you watch. She can play with your testicles or the shaft of your penis while you both go for a wild ride. This position can last a long time if you both have a lot of control. She can squeeze down on your penis with her pelvic muscles, or relax them to let you cool down so that you don't orgasm too quickly. You can rock forward and backward with your arms behind her back and slide in and out. Try using a cock ring with a bullet vibrator. Remember to turn the cock ring so that the bullet is on the side where it will touch her clitoris, or try a cock ring with two bullet vibrators on it. It will vibrate against the soft area at the base of your penis and your testicles for a totally new sensation while the other bullet is for her!

Reverse Cowgirl

©Akeim Ford

Then, there is the "reverse cowgirl" position. Now she is on top, but facing away from you. She can straddle you or have her legs wrapped around your thighs. Your penis is inside her in an entirely different direction. You and she can use your hands to wander everywhere while she pumps up and down on you, and you can enjoy the ride while watching her grind back and forth on you. In this picture, the woman has her legs wrapped around his legs for more clitoral friction. You can rub or scratch her back lightly, slap her on the rump for a little naughty spanking, and play with her breasts as she bobs up and down. Again, her clitoris is free to be played with for her to have a stronger orgasm from the combination of penetration and clitoral stimulation. You also have the option of adding some anal play while she wiggles her bum around while pleasuring both of you. (Make sure you have permission first—no knockin' on the back door without an invitation!) Make sure that you don't get hurt if she bends your penis in the wrong way or bounces too hard.

Man Standing Up

Try having your woman sit up on the edge of something that is countertop height (the bathroom vanity, the kitchen counter, or the bedroom dresser—you get the idea) and spread her legs. If you can enter her from a standing position, she can wrap her legs around your hips to pull you into her. Strong guys can even lift her off the surface and hold her while you pump away! She will be helping by wrapping her arms around your neck while she pulls you in deeper with her legs! If she is still sitting, wrap your arms under her knees and raise her legs higher for more penetration. Some women are flexible enough to place their legs on your shoulders for the maximum amount of penetration. Lift her buttocks with your hands and go for it. This position would also work with her against a wall, door, or in the shower. This is why we often talk about yoga… it gives you flexibility in the hip area so that you can try some of the more interesting positions.

©Akeim Ford

Entering Her from Behind

©Akeim Ford

Next is the famous "doggy style" where you enter her vagina from behind her. She can be kneeling, standing, or on her stomach with pillows under her belly to lift her pelvis up toward you. Many couples are fond of this because it seems a little naughty, and you have a lot of options to add in as you wish. Reach under her and play with her clitoris. Or let HER use her hand or a vibrator to stimulate her clitoris.

©Akeim Ford

This variation, with both of you in a kneeling position, gives you both the pleasure of being hands free and the power of your legs and hips to control the level of penetration.

Side-to-Side Sex

©Akeim Ford

Side-to-side sex is great for people with bad backs. You can be face-to-face or you enter her from behind her. You still have one hand free to play with her; you can kiss her neck and shoulders or give some love bites while you and she rock together to climax. She may want you to touch her clitoris at the same time. You can use this position for anal sex, too...to give your back and upper body a break. You can try different leg positions that are physically feasible and comfortable. Done face-to-face, the side-to-side position is very connecting and recommended for a deep, intimate sexual encounter.

Face to Face Sitting

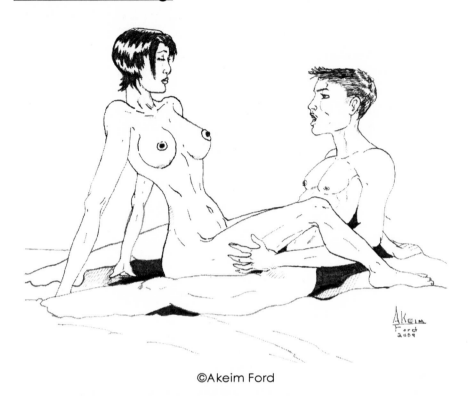

©Akeim Ford

Engaging in intercourse while facing each other in a sitting position is both intimate and erotic. Many people find this position in line with Tantric and Taoist sexual philosophies because the movements are more of a rocking together sensation and can allow for more genital-to-genital contact. It also allows for intimate kissing and mutual hand freedom for touching and stimulation. Also, it can be used to slow down the urgency for a man to ejaculate while still keeping an erection and stimulating the most sensitive parts of the woman's vagina. Lastly, it is a great position for the pregnant woman, as she can control penetration without any weight on her protruding belly. Sex doesn't have to stop during pregnancy—see our chapter on pregnancy later on in this book!

Well, by now it should be clear that the missionary position is just a starting point for the pleasures that intercourse can provide. Our best advice: experiment with your sex play and keep it fresh and exciting. If you find that you and your partner fall into a habit of having sex in the same position most of the time, make a commitment to try a new position at least once a week. You might even want to make it a special regular night—like Friday is new sex position night! Or maybe a weekend morning—the breakfast of champions! Creativity is the key to keeping your sex life from getting stale. No worries! You are a Love Warrior, and being sexually adventurous is in your nature...

CHAPTER 16.
Toys—Not Just For Kids Anymore!

Dildos and vibrators and butt plugs…Oh my! There are so many options and so many unanswered questions. Many men cringe at the thought of using toys because they believe that they will be replaced by a mechanical device. This is historically not true. Most women, especially those who have been single for long periods, will tell you that they enjoy using a vibrator or dildo during masturbation. Why? Because it feels good, hits all the right spots, you get to control the speed, depth of penetration; you get to choose the design of the toy or toys, and a host of other reasons based on newer technology of the toys and their purposes. And, there are hundreds of toys for men too! From sleeve masturbators to cock rings and anal plugs, the only thing stopping you from running out to the store and stocking up is deciding where to start. Of course, the second thing stopping a lot of guys is that they go to the local toy store and freak out when they are greeted by much younger salespeople and are surrounded by some huge dildos hanging from the ceiling, banging into their heads.

Hence the reason we chose to open an online adult toy store…to give you a safe place to peruse through the most preferred and best made products with all of the information that you need to make your shopping experience a comfortable one for you and your partner. At www.LoveHerRightStore.com, we educate you about what toys are good for what purposes, what lubes to choose, and how to keep your toys clean, safe, and out of sight of the little ones. **We have also made sure that all the toys we picked are phthalate free to ensure your good health today and tomorrow.**

So, where do you start? Most women would say that their favorite toys involve ones that have clitoral stimulators. They offer you so many options, including portability if you go on a vacation and don't want to pack your whole bag of tricks.

Clitoral vibrators have many forms. Some are shaped like rabbits and dolphins; some are more artistically designed to be less obvious if left out on the bedside accidently. They may have a single speed vibrator bullet, or may have multiple speeds for varying intensities (Yummy!). Some are attached to cock rings, which we will cover in a little while, and some are attached to dildos. One by LELO even looks like a lipstick and can be charged up by plugging it into your computer USB port.

So what's the big deal? Ask a woman who likes the varying sensations and she might tell you that while you are engaging in intercourse, the additional use of a clitoral vibrator will not only get her to climax with your penis inside her, which is very difficult to do without clitoral stimulation, but that when she climaxes, she will squeeze down on you and make your climax more intense too. Pick an intercourse position, add a vibrator between you, and you have serious fun for you both. Also, if you are tired, she can use a vibrator on herself, giving you an opportunity to watch her climax. Or, she can put on a show while she masturbates and you manually stimulate her internally if you both feel like it. Or, if she is on top, one of you can be using the vibrator on her while she rides you. Clitoral vibrators are starting to sound a little more interesting, eh?

Toys—Not Just For Kids Anymore!

The most important thing to understand about all sexual toys is the material they are made of. It has been found that inexpensive toys may have a chemical in them called phthalates. Many of these unsafe sex toys are made out of jelly rubber. Phthalates have been proven to be carcinogenic over time, so for the health of you and your partner, shop wisely and invest in toys that are of high quality. You will also find that higher-quality toys are made of various cool materials used to simulate skin and provide more sensitivity. Our favorite line of beautifully made and designed vibrators and internal stimulators for women and men is LELO. Many of their products are made of cyberskin, which is amazingly like human skin and feels more natural when being used. Their designs are works of art, and they don't look like sex toys, so you won't want to crawl under the bed if the kids stumble upon them! They also have a manufacturer's warranty of one year, which is almost unheard of in the sex toy industry, so they are worth the investment.

Dr. Joni: The next section discusses toys and techniques many of you may not be familiar with, including toys for him. You may choose not to read it; the choice is yours. Sexuality is what you make it, just have a discussion with your partner about what makes each of you feel good and try something new once in a while. The things you enjoy you can repeat!

Dildos and vibrators

Any toy made of rubber is porous and cannot be totally sterilized once used. Rubber sometimes contains latex or phthalates, softeners used in production. Any person with chemical sensitivities and latex allergies should also avoid jelly rubber. Store rubber toys by themselves; their material may react to other rubbers and plastics. Or, choose another product such as silicone, cyberskin, glass, or stainless steel. Make sure that you have bought an appropriate toy cleaner; soap alone will not work. Make sure that the lubricant is appropriate for the material of the toy. Latex dildos can be used safely on a latex-sensitive person if covered with a nonlatex condom, but why bother if you can just buy one made out of a safer product? A vaginal latex allergy reaction is going to put you in the doghouse for a week to ten days, and you may be spending some time in the emergency room trying to explain to the doctors and nurses that you were fooling around with a latex toy. Pretty embarrassing for you and painful for her!

Toys made of glass and stainless steel sound a little clinical and maybe even painful, but they offer some advantages. They can be made hot or cold to change the sensation, and they are the safest to use from a cleanliness perspective. On the other hand, they do not bend and curve to fit inside the body, so they have limitations. Sometimes, you have to try one or two different types before you discover what you both enjoy.

NEVER USE A DILDO IN HER ANUS AND THEN IN HER VAGINA!

So why do you need a dildo or vibrating dildo when you have a perfectly wonderful penis to insert inside of her? Again, use your imagination! Imagine performing oral sex on your partner while you insert a dildo or vibrating dildo inside of her. She will be screaming at the wonderfully powerful sensations of the multiple places that you can reach with both. You can be licking her clitoris and massaging her G-Spot simultaneously, and she can be brought to multiple orgasms in the process. Or, she may want some anal penetration with oral sex. Butt plugs are made specifically for that purpose. They are not too long, have a handle, so that it does not get lost inside of you (another embarrassing trip to the ER), and they can be used on men and women.

For now, let's stay on the topic of dildos and vibrating dildos. Again, if you just want to kiss and fondle her and touch her, bring out a vibrator or a dildo. There are special straps that wrap around your thigh or chest that the dildo attaches to, and the toy can be inside of her while she plays with you.

You can be in a 69 position, happily licking away at each other, while she still gets the sensation of the penetration of the dildo. You can also pick the size and diameter of the dildo (OOOOH AAAH!!!). Just because your penis is perfect in every way, some women may need or want something a little bigger or thicker. It does not mean that you are not sufficient size-wise…it is just for variety. Similarly, you might want a tighter sensation against your penis shaft, and there are vaginal tightening sprays to make her get that virgin-tight feeling that she used to have before children. Check out the Intimate Organics Embrace Vaginal Tightening Gel (Beware: other tightening sprays and gels use alum, which is very drying and unsafe. Intimate Organics uses only certified organic ingredients; this product uses a derivative of the pepper plant. It is temporary, totally safe, and has no side effects.)

Anal play for men…a new frontier. Many men like the sensation of being anally penetrated. No, you are not gay if you find this enjoyable. Men have a spot near the prostate gland called the P spot that many men find to be pleasurable when stimulated. You can add clitoral and penis stimulation at the same time for intimate sex play. Some women will use a harness and dildo and enter a man from behind and use the other hand to stroke the man's penis at the same time. It is your time to play, and trying different toys and positions will bring your relationship from dull to mind blowing!

Or, you can choose to play with anal beads and plugs. Anal beads are an interesting toy, as they can be inserted, then slowly, one by one, pulled out to tease and heighten your pleasure and add to the surprise element of your sexual playtime. They can be used on both men and women. Anal plugs may vibrate or not, and some are made for simultaneous vaginal and anal insertion. Again, lubrication is a must, as the anus does not create its own lubrication and insertion has to be slow and gentle until you find the right pace and pleasure zones. (We will be discussing back door play in greater detail in an upcoming chapter.)

So how can we forget about cock rings? We can't because they serve a variety of purposes. They are made of a material, usually rubber, silicone, or stainless steel that fits around the base of the penis and puts pressure on the shaft of the penis. This not only feels good to you, but it keeps the blood flow inside the penis shaft and helps to give you a stronger, harder erection. This is especially helpful if you are having trouble staying hard enough, or you just want some extra reassurance for your lasting power. Some cock rings have vibrating bullets in them, usually one or two. There may be some pleasure nubs for stimulating you or her. With the vibrating bullets you both have options as to where you might want a little vibration action; her clitoris, your testicles, your or her perineum, or all of the above depending on the toy. You can turn them on or off, or increase the speed if one of you needs more sensation. These help when she wants you inside of her and hand action is difficult, but her clitoris is begging for stimulation. They usually work using batteries, but some of the newer vibrating toys are rechargeable and have locking mechanisms so that they do not activate inside of your suitcase, which will ensure you a trip to the back room with a TSA person if it is in your carry-on.

Toys—Not Just For Kids Anymore!

There are so many varieties of vibrators that we could write books just on the variations, but we want to mention just a few more for your consideration.

- Vibrating tongue rings (great for oral sex)
- Fingertip vibrators
- Penis enhancement sleeves (slides over your penis to give you more size, girth or length, while you are still penetrating her with your own penis)

Lubricants and what goes with what:
- When in doubt, use a water-based lubricant. It is the closest to her natural pH and secretions. If you are having sex in the shower or tub and using a silicone toy, then please use a silicone-based lube because the water-based lubes will wash away in the water. You may use either water- or silicone-based lubes with glass or stainless steel toys.
- Don't forget to try some stimulating lubricants for fun for you and her. There are clitoral stimulating gels, G-Spot gels, flavored gels for him and her, penis size enhancement creams, and vaginal tightening sprays. Variety is the spice of life; have a sense of adventure and see what turns you on!
- For anal play, lubrication is a must, as our bodies do not naturally create any anal lubrication. In addition, we recommend trying an anal-relaxing product to relax the muscles before playing. Our favorites are the Intimate Organics Daring or Adventurous Anal Sprays since they enhance your experience naturally by relaxing the sphincter muscles using natural products, rather than numbing the anus. Many other commercial brands of

anal relaxation products use lidocaine, which is an anesthetic. If it hurts, you really want to know so that you do not cause tearing of the very delicate anal tissue—you should stop at that point.

There are literally thousands of toy options to consider and enjoy! Talk to your partner and decide what toy you would like to experiment with first. Then, as you get more adventurous, you might want to try a different type of toy. Toys are also a great way to make an adult night of playing an adult sex-related game like "Synchrohearts" or "Discover Your Lover." Light some candles and bring out the toys and lubes. Massage each other, play the game, and romp like kids with adult toys and games. Life should not be so serious, so try something new, fun, and sexy!

Connecting with your partner on an intimate, erotic level is the best gift that you can give to your relationship. Discover your partner's inner fantasies, see what you are willing to try, and give it a whirl! If you find that it isn't all that you thought that it would be, so what! Try, try again! Love on.

CHAPTER 17.
Becoming A Multiorgasmic Couple

It's true: most women do not put as much emphasis on penis size as they do with the girth (width), and your ability to know how deep and whether you should thrust quicker or slower. Average penis length is about six inches. Since you can't insert your entire length into your partner due to things that get in the way, like bellies, or certain positions, what really counts is how you use it. Most thrusting techniques are the obvious in and out, but the Taoists 3000 years ago had medical reasons and sexual techniques that were prescribed for sexual healing and enhanced sexual pleasure. They described certain parts of the vagina and penis that may be massaged for healing medical ailments. Basically, they had a philosophy that an orgasm a day keeps the doctor away!

Our favorite book that we refer to is the *Multi-Orgasmic Couple* by Mantak and Maneewan Chia and Doug and Rachel Abrams, MD. The book describes in detail how men and women can become multiorgasmic and how to use ancient techniques to transform your sex life. Yes, men can be multiorgasmic, but it takes a little learning and practice to separate a man's orgasm feeling from the actual ejaculatory phase. Men can have orgasms without ejaculating, which, according to the Taoists, drains your sexual energy so that you can't keep going. If you want to stop an ejaculation, you need to learn how to apply pressure using your PC muscles to apply pressure to the prostate gland, or to the head or base of the penis to stop the ejaculation from occurring. You still get all of the pleasure from the muscle contractions, which define your orgasm, but you don't emit semen. Yes, men can be multiorgasmic, but no one talks about it. This is how the Taoists believe that men can perform for a longer period of time and have more sexual satisfaction, while giving their partners more pleasure at the same time. This is especially useful for multiorgasmic couples, which we hope that you will strive to become. For an in-depth discussion and great exercises to help you become multiorgasmic too, please get a copy of *The Multi-Orgasmic Man* by Mantak Chia and Douglas Abrams.

The first part that is emphasized is that you never have intercourse unless your female partner is highly aroused. It is recommended that she have at least one orgasm before intercourse. **The Taoist believe that foreplay should last at least thirty minutes before intercourse to allow the female "yin" energy to get to a high enough level for total sexual satisfaction.** You can get her aroused by all of the methods that we have described so far, plus a few moves of your own, which we hope that you have developed by now. The ultimate scenario is when man and woman have an energy give and take, like a rollercoaster, where your sexual energy is going back and forth between you as you enjoy the pleasure of your lovemaking session. **Intercourse lovemaking should last about thirty minutes as well, in order to allow both partners to have time to be completely satisfied!**

During the intercourse phase of lovemaking, there are basically three types of thrusting movements that are described:

- Shallow Thrusts
- Long Deep Thrusts
- Short Deep Thrust

Shallow Thrusts

Shallow thrusting is the best for stimulating a woman's sensitive outer third of the vagina, where the G-Spot is located. This motion is sensually stimulating to both the man and woman, touching the head of the penis and the woman's sensitive zones simultaneously. It might encourage the man to want to ejaculate, so alternate among the motions to allow for orgasms without ejaculation for him, while giving orgasms to her!

Long Deep Thrusts

Long, deep thrusts are stimulating to both partners. How to best do this is to start by drawing back your penis almost out of her vagina to her vaginal entrance between thrusts. You are getting the shaft of the penis stroked, and she is getting the head of your penis stimulating her sensitive vaginal zones. These thrusts are also useful if you are having trouble maintaining an erection.

Short Deep Thrusts

This is done when the man is staying deep inside of the woman and is rocking his pelvis forward and back. This gives more chances for her clitoris to rub against your pubic bone, and you don't get as much stimulation to your penis head. This will help control ejaculation, especially if your woman is having an orgasm with you inside of her and you don't want to fall over the cliff by ejaculating so that you can continue having intercourse. This rocking back and forth movement with you deep inside of her is a very connecting and harmonizing motion, which can calm you both down, enabling you to hit a plateau before climbing another wave of sexual excitement.

Rhythm

Thrusting rhythm is something that you have to find that works best for both of you at each encounter. Taoists suggest nine shallow thrusts and one long deep thrust as the most pleasurable for both partners, and you can still control your ejaculation. The key is to experiment with depth, direction, and speed. If you can maintain control over your ejaculation, you can use fewer shallow thrusts and then a short deep thrust and then a long deep thrust.

Really Screwing

The term screwing was defined 3000 years ago! Who knew? It has a completely different connotation from what we see and think of when we see couples banging in and out of each other while having intercourse. The term screwing involves using your tailbone to guide your hip thrusts as you thrust in and out of your partner. Think about making half circles with your penis, first in one direction and then in the other. You will be stimulating parts of each of you that a simple in-and-out motion will not touch! In Tao language, when you are really screwing, it is like the difference between a nail and a screw. The nail will come out easily, while the screw will stay in for a longer period of time. At first, your movements may come more from your hip area instead of your sacrum. You can feel your sacrum if you put one hand on your pubic bone and one hand on your tailbone between your buttocks. Using this screwing motion enhances the sensations during penetration for both of you, while controlling the levels of arousal at the same time...COOL!

Getting Close To The Edge

If you think that your excitement level is getting too hot and you want to delay ejaculation, pause your thrusting. Take a couple of deep breaths, let your sexual level drop a little, and use short, deep thrusts until you are back in control. Of course, if your partner or you are tired from having so many orgasms or want to go to sleep, then let it rip and allow yourself to ejaculate!

Three thousand years ago, Taoist physicians figured out what the best positions are, how to use them, how to become multiorgasmic as a man, and why sex is so healthy for you! Who are we to question three thousand years of data? Learning how to tune into the energy between you and your partner during one of the most intimate partner pleasures might bring your lovemaking skills and satisfaction to new levels.

CHAPTER 18.

Coloring Outside The Lines: Become Each Other's Fantasy

Please take note: When you read this section, please understand that if you are not comfortable with this topic, then skip it. Maybe there will be another time that you might consider reading this section. We want to address issues that we have seen and been asked about, and answer questions about things that some of our readers may be curious about. We are daring to go where few dare to tread in order to take away the mystery of what some people consider to be normal for them!

We want to start this segment by stating that you and your partner get to decide how your relationship is going to progress. Fantasies are normal, and acting on them is also normal. In fact, we don't even put limitations on what we consider fantasy or fetish and where to draw the lines. In our relationship, we choose to stay monogamous because we have learned to become each other's fantasies with role playing and other means.

Sex Outside the Bedroom

There is something terribly naughty about the dangers of being caught in a sexual position that isn't the missionary position behind closed bedroom doors. Having said that, beware that if you get caught having sex in public places you will be charged by the police—not a mad turn-on. Many people find just the concept of getting caught (by the neighbors, the kids, strangers, the cops, etc.) unbelievably sexy. Our advice: bust open the bedroom doors and plan a seduction elsewhere. Start with other rooms of the house, maybe when the kids are out.

Try the shower—it's a great alternative while the kids are in front of a video, and it's the most popular place for couples with kids to have sex. Sex in the shower is a wondrous experience! While you are both wet and soapy, offer to wash her hair and wash her all over, touching her whole body; feel the difference in the softness of her skin on different parts of her body. You can slide all over each other and kiss your way into mad, passionate sex. You might want to keep some lube in the shower for a quickie. For use with toys, use a silicone lube, since a water-based one will wash away. If you can't figure out how to grab the grout lines with your toes, try the most fabulous products we have: **Sex In The Shower**! Check out our online adult shopping site www.LoveHerRightStore.com for this incredible new line. In addition to the hot and sexy packaging, this line has everything you need to make your shower experience amazing! The line includes handles, footrests, and handcuffs that attach to your shower or tub using heavy duty suction cups, so they're not permanent, and they're portable, for great sex in the shower at home or away! They also have vibrating sponges, a double headed massaging showerhead, and waterproof toys—everything you could possibly need to relocate your passion to the bathroom! **Sex In The Shower** will have you panting to get wet!

You can also try other rooms of the house (kitchen counters, the washing machine or dryer, chairs, or any horizontal or vertical surface that can theoretically support your weight and gets you both at the right height level in case you are much taller than she is). (You'll never look at the kitchen the same way again!) Just don't break the furniture! Well, if you do, you will have quite the story to brag about! Be sure to place a pillow or towel under her if the surface is hard, so that she doesn't get black and blue marks on her butt.

If you decide to try getting sexy outside, please be aware that you are doing an illegal act and that it's possible to get noticed by the police. They do not have much of a sense of humor for indecent exposure...Don't get caught! (We are officially absolved of any responsibility if you get arrested....)

Here's a sexy idea: try manually stimulating each other in the ocean. It's easier than trying to have intercourse in the water and trying to camouflage that. No one knows what you're doing, and it's a whole new way to enjoy the beach!

Dressing Up and Role-Playing

Wearing women's clothing, anal sex, fetish sex, and restraints are not considered "normal" by some. We challenge that and want to reveal what other people are doing and how. We'll wager that some of you have had thoughts about some of these sexual practices, maybe even fantasized or tried some in private. If it's not your thing, that's all right by us. Lingerie is a great way to look and feel sexy, and now there are many kinds of lingerie for him and her in a wide variety of styles and sizes. Everyone has the right to feel sexy for themselves and for their partners.

Sometimes, couples can play out their fantasies with role playing. Think about it as dressing up and acting out your fantasies while your lover fills in the role of your fantasy. Costumes, props, toys, silk scarves, ropes, paddles, even handcuffs are all part of their sex toy box for many people. Do you have a French maid fantasy? Give it a shot!

Once you are very intimate with each other, you will discover that your relationship is a safe place to indulge each other's fantasies. Maybe she likes the idea of coming onto you while you're cleaning the pool—her little pool boy can come inside for a dip in her pool! Or you can incorporate household chores into a fantasy! You can even make whole dates out of a fantasy: "Do you always entertain when your husband is out of town?" Have a picnic on the bed. This is only a fun thing when there is absolutely no threat of any cheating...ever. This is about monogamy, passion, and love, and open-minded fantasy can play a healthy role as long as you both understand that this only works when only the two of you are involved.

Why do you think *Playboy* and the rest of the sex industry stays in business? Remember that your biggest sex organ is between your ears, and when you are getting laid, you probably won't care how you got there, as long as it feels good! Tell us that you don't have a couple of fantasies that you think about while you jerk off, and we'll tell you that you're a liar. It's NORMAL to fantasize, and we think it's normal to act them out!

So what is a fetish? What is taboo? Is it wrong if you like to wear women's underwear or lingerie? In Provincetown, Massachusetts, they have a yearly event for straight men who like to dress like women. It is called Fantasia Fair and is very popular. Men come to town with their wives or partners and can dress on the outside how they feel like on the inside, and they can feel safe. They are sharing this with their partners, and everybody is happy and gets their sexual needs fully met. It may not be your thing, but it works for them, so why not let them be happy?

Erotic Film (Porn)

Historically, porn has been a big taboo because of the naughtiness about watching other people having sex.

In addition, porn has historically depicted women in a degrading way, all about male pleasure only. That said, today's porn industry is more mature, providing options for couples to enjoy erotic films while showing all of the characters happily engaging in sexual acts and having sexual satisfaction. This is an opportunity to discover whether porn works for you as erotic stimulation. It's also worth mentioning that just because there are types of porn that turn you on (like same-sex porn or sex with anonymous partners), it doesn't mean that you want to go out and do those things! You are still with your partner doing sexy things together!

The other opportunity that exists is the whole genre of educational videos. Learn about new sexual techniques with video assistance, which also provides a subconscious level of permission to watch this type of erotic film, watching others have sex in the name of education. School was never this much fun! Visit our store Web site for a great selection of educational videos that will definitely be a whole new version of postgraduate study! This whole conversation is about incorporating more tools to live a more erotic existence. Erotic films can assist in doing just that.

Anal Sex

What if you like having anal sex? Is that a fantasy or a fetish, or is it something to think about trying? Many men want to perform anal penetration on their female partners. It is a different sensual experience for you, since your penis will feel more constriction and the whole conversation is a little "naughty." First, talk about it—going in the back door uninvited is not a turn-on! Second, be sure that she is turned on enough, meaning she has had several orgasms already so she is really into this extension of sex play. Third, be sure to use an anal-relaxing spray (be careful which one you choose). Please beware that most anal products are made with lidocaine, which is an anesthetic—bad idea! Using these types of products deadens the nerves, which blocks your pain sensors. This can result in tearing. Please avoid these types of products; they cause more harm than good. Our best recommendation is made by Intimate Organics, called Organic Adventure Anal Spray for Women, which you can find at our store site in the Anal Play Section. We like this product because it uses absolutely no lidocaine, so her sphincter muscles are naturally relaxed without deadening the nerves and blocking pain response. You want her to be able to ask you to slow down so no one gets hurt.

*If you have a very large penis, or if your body types are opposite—you're a big guy and she has a much smaller build—bear in mind that anal sex may be uncomfortable or impossible for her to enjoy. Have a serious discussion first, and be sure that she's amenable to trying it.

It is very important to use a lot of lubrication; the anus does not create its own lubrication like the vagina does. Intimate Organics also makes a great water-based lube that we adore. Start with a well-lubed finger, and be sure she is ready for more before you progress. Enter very slowly until her sphincter relaxes, and let her start to set the pace. Make sure that you never go from a woman's anus to her vagina because transferred bacteria will cause her to get a vaginal infection. So, take a break and wash your hands or penis REALLY well or use a condom for anal sex and change it before proceeding to the next course. Anal play can be messy, so try the shower if you have a concern about the messy factor, or keep dark towels on hand for the bed, so you won't notice it.

Now, what about **you**, big man? Ever thought about having anal sex performed on you? In some couples, the woman may use a dildo and penetrate her man, or they make butt plugs designed for anal pleasure. Some have vibrators in them too. Well, guess what? Men have a G-Spot too! On men it is referred to as the P-Spot. It just happens to be located in the area of the prostate, which is inside your anus. Yep, it is up your ass, and some guys have their hottest orgasms while receiving a blow job and using a butt plug or dildo in their bottom at the same time. Don't knock it until you have tried it. Again, we would advise using lots of lube and an anal relaxing spray, like Intimate Organics Daring Anal Spray for Men. Start small with a finger first and have your partner slide inside you slowly, and gently move in and out of you while she gives you a hand or blow job at the same time. Don't forget to buy a good toy cleaner that kills bacteria if you use toys for anal play. Toy cleaners should be a part of your sex toy box anyway with all toys.

This act is about sharing a very intimate part of you, exposing a private part of yourself to your partner. Take that charge seriously, with responsibility, and honor it. You want to make this a pleasurable experience for you both. You can also combine anal play with oral play, which can make for an intense experience for either of you. This is also a wonderful opportunity to entrust your partner with all of you, which allows you an incredible level of freedom and deepens the intimacy and bond between you.

Sex involving other people

We are not so naïve to believe that everyone will make the same choices we have. Some couples choose to engage in swinging, swapping, or threesomes. *If you choose to bring other people into your sexual relationship, please make sure that you have clear communication and mutual*

agreements. We don't want to see relationships break up from jealousy or worse—diseases.

So what if your partner asked you if you would consider doing a threesome? Most guys would love to watch two women getting it on, right? What role would you play in the threesome? How do you pick this person? Who gets to pick? Who gets to do what to whom? How do you decide? These are just some of the questions that you need to consider before you start shopping for another sex partner to fit the bill. If you think that this is getting complicated, we're just getting started.

Many couples have open relationships. This means that they are allowed to sleep with other people, and their partner has said that it is OK and that they can too. Sometimes, one person has the need to have other lovers more than the other. Can you do this and not get jealous? The first conversation you better have is with yourself. If you are the jealous type, you will probably have problems with your relationship at some point if you enter into this agreement. If you and your partner can accept that it is just sex and not really love, then you may be able to handle it. This is where our ever-present conversation about communication comes in or you will be walking down a path to disaster that you have allowed. The same thing applies to having threesomes. We have had couples ask us this question because one of the partners is bisexual and they want to have all of their needs met. If your woman wants to be with another woman and you get to watch, are you OK with this or will you feel left out? Sometimes you never know until you are in the middle of the threesome and realize that you might have made a mistake. Now what?

The most important thing to do is have this conversation with your partner and decide on all of the agreements and answer the questions that we put to you in the beginning. Then, the final question is...what happens if you realize that it is not comfortable and that one of you feels that your relationship will be compromised? You have to make sure that your relationship with your partner is **the** most important thing in the world and that you will **BOTH** fight for it to stay that way.

So, if you decide to act out a fantasy with a threesome, please, please, PLEASE practice safer sex. No orgasm is worth getting sick or dying over. **<u>Don't bring home diseases from someone else</u>**! That one is hard to forgive, even in an open relationship. That means using condoms for oral sex and penetration and using rubber dams, also called dental dams, to have oral sex on a female stranger. Or don't engage in those practices. Too many people have died from unprotected sex. AIDS and other sexually trans-mitted diseases (STDs) do not discriminate and can be prevented. If you are going to have oral sex performed on you by a stranger, use a nonlubricated condom. You don't know who that person has been with and who they were with. It goes on and on until you realize that every time you sleep with a different person, you are sleeping with an army of unknown disease carriers.

Now you understand why we practice and endorse monogamy. It is just too complicated for us to have to think about licking latex and who everybody has been with. Even the most professional-looking, clean people may have been exposed and can carry the AIDS virus for ten years without it being detected. Please choose your life together carefully and take time to recheck your agree-ments with your partner to make sure that everything is still working for both of you. Your relationship depends on it, and it deserves to be honored.

Dominance and Submission

Sometimes you might like to get a little spanking while having sex or as part of foreplay. Another option might be for one of you to hold the other's hands above the head, or behind the back, or consider trying the use of restraints: handcuffs or scarves for a little domination/ submission role-playing. This adds a little fantasy into the scene. Maybe tie a silk scarf over her eyes so she doesn't know what you will do to her next; the anticipation may drive her wild! Just make sure that she is OK with giving up control first; then, let the games begin! Her senses will be heightened, and the anticipation of not knowing where your hands, mouth, or penis will go next is a juicy turn-on. There are lots of toys for these kinds of games, from the tame to the exotic, including paddles, ticklers, and whips that range from feathers to leather to give you different sensations and intensities.

Remember, you never want to try something new without communication and feeling safe. If you do, you may never get another chance to try something else new or different. Also, have a "safe" word, and use it whenever your partner or you get into a place where it may become psychologically or physically uncomfortable and you need a quick way to get the message across that what you are doing is not working for one of you. **Safe words are a mandatory halt signal.** Pick a word that you wouldn't be using in conversation, so there is no mistaking it! Don't forget, because hand signals won't work if your hands are tied!

*(If you are using restraints, please use cuffs with quick releases or Velcro so that if someone gets that "I am feeling out of control and I want out NOW!" feeling, he or she can do so quickly.)

Some people think of this as S&M. We prefer to use the words domination and submission. You get to label it, not us. We are strong believers that sex between two consenting adults is up to you to define. What goes on behind closed doors is not for us to judge. This is why we always tell our audience that we are a safe place to ask these delicate questions because "traditional" teachings and some religious persons have told you that these are "dirty" or "sinful" acts.

We do not agree. So we're heathens and may burn in hell, but we will have had a lot of hot fun in the meantime, and we'll see some of you there too! Who's bringing the handcuffs?

> Here's an idea: combine sexy foods and a little naughty play. Plan a food seduction where the pre-foreplay involves a scarf and different types of finger foods. See if she can identify the foods without seeing them.

Suggestions:
1. Keep some dark-colored towels under the bed to minimize who gets to sleep in the wet spot. Also useful if you have sex during your woman's menstrual cycle, or decide to try anal play.
2. Create your personal "Sex Toy Box." Keep it close to the bed so that you may reach into it without delaying your playing, and keep lubes, toys, massage products, etc. in it so that the kids can't find your love tools.
3. Make love after a shower. You are more likely to have oral sex or want to give her oral sex on her clean, sweet-smelling body.
4. Try something different at least once every two weeks. It will keep your sex life hot and unpredictable. Create a box with little pieces of paper with your fantasies in it. Pull one out and try it!
5. Make a date to shop for toys, lingerie, or sexy DVDs together. You will be amazed at what is new and hot for you to consider trying.

Check out our store site at www.LoveHerRightStore. com. We have personally picked the best of what is available, affordable, and safe to use. Cheaply made toys may have phthalates in them, which are cancer-causing agents! None of our products contain phthalates, and we are proud and pleased to help our Love Her Right family by providing only safe and fun toys! We also guide you as to what we think are the best toy cleaners, lubes, massage products, etc.

6. Consider taking one of our Love Warrior Challenges and transform your relationship. By making passion a daily commitment, you are telling your partner that recreating your life together as a more passionate existence is worthy of dedication. Try it and see how your whole world changes!

There are lots of varieties of sexual experience to consider trying together. Boredom in the bedroom will lead to having less sex, and we don't want that to happen. It doesn't have to happen as far as we are concerned. We want you to have sex in every room of your house in lots of positions and on lots of flat surfaces or sturdy chairs! Do it often, and savor all of the sensations that the human body is capable of. Study after study shows us that sexually fulfilled couples have the happiest and most successful relationships. Decide that you want to be one of them, and become a Love Warrior to whatever level of adventure you choose together, for today and forever.

CHAPTER 19.
Staying Lovers For A Lifetime

"Age does not protect you from love.
But love, to some extent, protects you from age."

—Jeanne Moreau, actor and writer

For great sex until the day we die, we need to focus on several things: our health, our definition of a sexual encounter, and how to handle the changes that inevitably happen to our bodies as we age...and manage those changes as a couple. In all the research we have done, the most enlightening and informative resources have been the Taoist teachings concerning sexuality. While much of the Western-based research is helpful, the differences lie in how this ancient philosophy talks about maintaining your sexual fire without drugs. By using different positions and techniques, everyone truly can strive to be sexual for a lifetime!

Esther: Our favorite book on Taoist sexuality is The Multi-Orgasmic Couple by Maneewan and Mantak Chia and Douglas and Rachel Abrams. The Chia couple are Taoist sexuality practitioners, and

Rachel Abrams is a Western doctor, so the book has an amazing amount of vital information from both perspectives. It is a must for your erotic library! You can find it on our Web site, or any online or brick-and-mortar bookstore.

One of the major attractions of Taoist sexuality teachings is that it is rooted in monogamy and teaching how to create a life-long, vibrant sexual relationship. Taoists say that it takes seven years to know your partner's body, seven years to know your partner's mind, and seven years to know your partner's spirit. So, you have a long time to become a true Love Warrior!

According to Taoist tradition, one of the easiest ways to maintain a vibrant sexual relationship is to stay healthy and, like any other muscle group, you have to use it or lose it! Sex is like any other part of your health—the better you take care of your sexuality, the better your sexuality will take care of you. Having sex, and having it as often as possible, is the easiest way to guarantee that your golden years will be red hot too! The Taoists recommend having sex (to climax) a minimum of once a week as we age to keep all of our sex hormones flowing and our parts in working order. There's an added benefit: because of the way our hormones work—especially our old friend oxytocin—the more sex we have, the more feel-good hormones we produce, so the more sex we want. How's that for a fabulous cycle! Beware that the opposite is also true: the longer you go without being sexual, the easier it is to lose that connection with your sexual self.

Here's another cool tidbit. As we age, our bodies inevitably change (Please read the chapters on menopause and Low T/ED. The information is vital!) One of the cool things to look forward to is that after menopause, concerns about preventing pregnancy vanish, so spontaneity can become your new best friend. Also, as your testosterone levels decrease with age, your partner has the opposite happening—in comparison to her now rapidly declining estrogen levels, her testosterone levels, relatively speaking, are higher than before menopause. What does that mean for you? It means, according to Taoist tradition, that she is becoming more yang (more like fire), and you are becoming more yin (more like water). In Western words, she is going to have greater desire levels than before, and you may want to cuddle more and be more affectionate; you may take a little longer to arouse than when you were in your twenties. This is a good thing. Hormonally, men and women become more compatible as they age, and that is what the Golden Years should really be about!

The best reasons we found for having a vibrant sex life as we age were the surprises about improving your overall health. Study after study has shown that having an orgasm at least twice a week or more helps prevent breast cancer, helps you heal faster after illnesses (especially cancer), prevents premature aging, is great for your heart and your genitals, and lowers your stress levels as compared to people who don't have as much sex. This is true for both women and men, so stick with our motto of "An orgasm a day" for as long as you can, and if that gets to be too demanding physically, be sure to maintain at least two orgasms per week. This can be done together or on your own using masturbation if life gets in the way.

The Waxing and Waning of Desire—How to Harmonize Your Sexual Energies

We bet you know this song: you want to get lucky but she "has a headache." None of us need to get older to understand that in many relationships, the levels of desire are not always on the same page. This can be due to exhaustion, hormone fluctuations, stress, and other life factors. What do you do if your desire levels are different? The

Taoists have known that when there is disharmony in the bedroom, there can never be harmony in the relationship. Resolving marital discord is essential for the well-being and happiness of your relationship as a whole. Anyone who has experienced a partner withholding sex after an argument knows that this is true! (Again, this is why we keep saying communication is so important. Your mother's wedding day recommendation "Never Go To Bed Angry" should be engraved over every marriage bed!) Taoist sexuality is not about the thrill of the new, but the thrill of the known, and our potential to know our partner is infinite since we are ever changing. Here are a few suggestions to reconcile those differences.

- **If you initiate sex, don't take your partner's lack of sexual energy personally or as a reflection of how attractive or desirable you are**. OK, we know this is tough to actually put into action. To make it easier, try to remember that sexual attraction has more to do with each person's individual level of sexual energy than it does with how attractive our partner is. Sexual energy is first and foremost generated in an individual's own body. Like any other aspect of our health, it must be exercised and maintained by each of us.
- **Asking for sex puts us in a vulnerable position, so never dismiss or shun your partner if you are not feeling sexual.** If we are not feeling sexual, it is our responsibility to convey our lack of desire to our partner with love and without hurt or shame.
- **If you are not interested in sex, don't simply roll over and go to sleep if you're not in the mood.** Convey your lack of desire, but share your love and affection. Embrace and kiss your partner before going to sleep.

- **If you're not sure how you feel, have sex.** No one should feel compelled or obligated to have sex when they don't want to, but many times we are just not in touch with our sexual energy. It's understandable that, with all the multiple responsibilities we shoulder, by the time we get to bed, what we really want is a good night's sleep. That said, if you make healing love, and if you have discovered the capacity to be multiorgasmic, you may find that this lovemaking session brings you closer and gives you a source of energy.
- **Choose an alternative time for lovemaking.** If sex is not in the cards when you want it, make a date for sex—maybe in the morning or over the weekend. Make a plan to satisfy your sexual appetite with the same planning and forethought you use to satisfy your physical appetite. You can also agree to go to bed earlier or carve out a specific time to be sexual.

How to Be Sexual Without "Having Sex"

Another secret about maintaining a vibrant sexuality as we age is the redefinition of the act of sex. Barry McCarthy, coauthor of *Men's Sexual Health*, among many other titles, recommends redefining healthy sexuality as "enhancing intimacy, pleasuring, and eroticism for mutual satisfaction." Part of the way we do that is to redefine what "sex" is to each of us as a couple. Taoist tradition looks at sexuality as a fluid dance, rich in multiple acts of giving and receiving pleasure. Sex does not have to be viewed as an Olympic sport, with the gold medal being the male ejaculatory orgasm at the end of intercourse. There are a host of ways to be sexual together that do not include intercourse, which is particularly helpful if one of you is feeling sexual and the other is not. Try these different ways to have a sexual encounter without intercourse to keep you intimate when one of you isn't as turned on.

- **Make Love with your mouth and/or hands.** Taoists believe that we can absorb sexual energy from our partners, so if you are not that turned on and your partner is feeling sexual, make love orally. Sexual energy is transmitted via the nipples, tongue, vagina, and penis, so don't be surprised if after making love to you, your partner might be more in the mood! (Just don't expect it—the surprise will be worth it!) Oral sex also give us an opportunity to explore our partner's genitals in a way that intercourse does not, so consider this another fact-finding mission—you're getting good at those!

- **Masturbate while in the arms of your lover.** It is high time to take masturbation out of the closet (or bathroom) and reclaim our right to be sexual, no matter what. When one of you may be out of commission due to health challenges, the opportunity to have a sexual release with the loving arms of your partner enveloping you will keep you close. This deep level of connection is vital during times of stress on your relationship, so be sure that you still connect sexually, even when circumstances make that challenging.

- **If your partner can't or won't hold you while you pleasure yourself, do it anyway.** Whether you can still lie together or if you have to get out of bed and go into another room, having a sexual release when you need one is the responsible and self-loving thing to do. If your partner didn't want to go to the gym or take a jog with you, would you forgo your exercise routine? Probably not, and you shouldn't forgo your sexual release either. Maintaining your sexual health is as important as diet and exercise, and it is your responsibility to do so for your own health and longevity.

- **Massage—it is better to give than to receive.** If your partner is not feeling sexual, ask for a massage. If she is not in the mood to rub you, offer to rub her. The touch factor is a crucial element to being in touch with our own sexual energy, so who knows where a massage may lead? Don't forget about our old friend oxytocin. Massage gives us a healthy boost, giving and receiving, so go for it and get both of your love juices flowing.

- **Touch me baby.** If even massage isn't in the cards, be sure to touch each other to connect. Kissing and gentle touching is a great way to release oxytocin, and it will keep you connected even when one of you is not feeling at all sexual.

Having Great Sex As We Age

Taoist tradition believes that true sexual power is about the ability to satisfy oneself and one's partner. This ability can increase over the course of a lifetime as we understand and adjust to the physiological changes that inevitably take place. For women, our levels of sexual pleasure expand as we age, as our hormone levels change, and we become free from concerns about preventing pregnancy. For men, the challenge becomes how to maintain eroticism, and their interest in sex and sexual pleasure as they age, especially if challenged with erectile difficulties. Studies prove that sex dissipates or disappears from long-term relationships *when the men stop being sexual*. (So much for the bellyaching about women not wanting enough sex!) Surveys also show that sexually active seniors are the happiest people—in their relationships and in their lives as a whole. So the challenge is to keep it sexy. For most men over fifty, and sometimes much younger, the need for more direct stimulation to the penis is necessary to achieve and maintain an erection. Don't freak out. This is normal. (The only time you should get concerned is if over 50 percent of the time, you cannot get or maintain an erection even when you are aroused; then, it is time to reread the chapter "Straight Talk for Him" and make an appointment with your doctor!) Here are some tips you and your partner can use to encourage Mr. Willie to come out and play.

- **First things first: Relax!** If you freak out when you are having trouble getting it up, what happens biologically is that your body starts pumping adrenaline—the flight or fight response kicks in. All that adrenaline is in direct competition with your sex hormones, and it will win. This response also forces blood away from the genitals—great idea if you were being chased by a lion, but not so great if you're trying to get hard! So relax, and try to harmonize with your partner's sexual energy.

- **Try to focus on something that turns you on.** Do you like lingerie, sex toys, or watching your wife touch herself? Ask for it, relax, and allow yourself to get turned on.

- **Focus on giving your partner pleasure.** Make love to your partner orally or with your hands. Allow her arousal to be contagious, and absorb some of her sexual energy; you will find it easier to get aroused.

- **Talk about your erection concerns.** Communicate with your partner that you may need more of her help. Her gentle support and more direct stimulation of your penis will help.

- **Taoists recommend the Soft Entry Technique.** This is man on top, with his fingers creating a ring of pressure around the base of the penis to encourage trapping the blood and using gravity to assist in forcing blood flow into the genitals. Then, encourage your penis into her vagina (be sure she is well lubricated and fully aroused), keeping your fingers around the base of the penis as long as you feel necessary. Another way to do this is to try using an artificial assistant: a cock ring. Made out of flexible silicone, rubber, or stainless steel, these constriction rings will do what your fingers would as described above and give you the freedom to use your hands elsewhere.

- **For some, the use of additional artificial assistance might be helpful.** Erection enhancement sleeves, a toy that lets you put your partially hard penis into a silicone version of yourself, will allow you to have intercourse and pleasure your partner, while feeling like the stud you are. On our Web site, you will find a whole section on sexual enhancements that includes cock rings, sleeves, stimulant creams, and herbal supplements that may assist in maintaining erections.

🌷 **If you are taking any prescription medications, do your research.** Over 200 medications have sexual side effects. If you discover that one of your drugs may be causing Mr. Willie's lack of attention span, call your doctor and become a fierce advocate for your sexual health. Take your partner with you, and find out what options you may have for alternative meds that don't have sexual side effects.

Becoming a Master of the Art of the Bedchamber

The secret to becoming a Love Warrior is remembering that you have a lifetime to explore each other physically, emotionally, and spiritually. Mastering the Art of the Bedchamber takes dedication to each other's pleasure and a true understanding of what each partner needs and wants to feel loved and sexually satisfied. Of course, what we each need and want will change over time as we age and our outer circumstances vary. This is the core of this adventure—dancing through life together and maintaining the deep love, delicious sense of humor, and level of play necessary to keep life interesting. When it comes to sex as time goes by, keep these points in mind to make sure your sex life stays as hot as you want it to.

- Be sure to have a sexual encounter at least once a week, whatever that means to you as a couple.
- Touch often to keep your hormonal juices flowing and your affection levels for each other high.

- Be sure you each get enough genital stimulation for successful sexual interaction. That means her lubrication levels are high enough for sex play, and your erection is at attention.
- Use other methods when necessary, like the soft entry technique or physical enhancements to help you along.
- Reduce your consumption of alcohol and quit smoking to keep your sexual health in prime condition.
- Maintain a sense of play in your lovemaking—this is the best part of sex!

The most important thing to remember is that lovemaking is about just that: making love. Use your newfound sexuality as a powerful and endearing way to show each other how your love for one another can change, evolve, and grow over time, but also that the crux of your love—its intensity, fire, and passion—will always remain constantly expanding.

Part Five: Life Happens—
How to Keep it Sexy

"There is a fountain of youth: it is your mind, your talents, the creativity you bring to your life and the lives of people you love. When you learn to tap this source, you will truly have defeated age."

—Sophia Loren, actor

CHAPTER 20.
Sex And Intimacy During Pregnancy

Probably one of the most amazing times during a couple's life together is the prospect of the arrival of a new addition to your family. For many, the reality that your love for each other has literally resulted in a physical manifestation (that your love has created life) is an awe-inspiring reality. Almost every first-time expectant parent gets philosophical and terrified about what kind of parent he or she will be. Add to that the stress a lot of men go through dealing with the changes in their blossoming bride, and you have the mixture for explosive division in your relationship. Here's the good news: if you go into pregnancy prepared for what to expect and armed with the knowledge of how you can be the most helpful, pregnancy can be a magical and bonding experience for your marriage. The only book out there for dads-to-be about what you will encounter and what you should do is *A Labor With Love* by Leon Scott Baxter. A father of two and a recognized romance guru, Leon provides you with valuable insight, awesome recommendations, and even a week-by-week understanding of what is happening during your pregnancy and what you should be prepared for. It is a must read for all expectant dads.

What the heck is happening?

OK, so you have found out that you are expecting a baby—get excited! Your woman is experiencing a lot of changes right now, including huge hormone shifts as her body changes gears and begins the task of supporting a new life. She may be moody, irritable, moved to tears easily, and emotional. On a physical level, her body may be wreaking havoc. In addition to the hormone swings, she is probably dealing with waves of intense nausea, throwing up, and frequent urination. Her body is no longer her own or under her control, so emotionally she is probably freaking out. She needs your love, support, and excitement about this pregnancy. Remember when we talked about oxytocin? Well, now is oxytocin's big number. This is the hormone that also bonds mom to baby, and her brain is flooded with it, so she needs you emotionally and physically. Touch her, hug her, kiss her, pet her, and cuddle with her as often as you can. She needs to feel close to you, and this closeness is good for your relationship.

The first trimester of her pregnancy is rough, as her body adjusts to its new role. By the second trimester, things change again…for the better. Now, her hormones may be more in control, and her nausea and throwing up should be subsiding. Here is where things can get fun again, if you are prepared mentally and physically for things to be a little different, and you can maintain your sense of adventure and your sense of humor!

Pregnancy and Sexual Intimacy

OK, before you start freaking out, we are going to dispel a few myths. First, the baby **cannot** feel the act of you having intercourse, so those of you that are afraid the baby will have a dent in the middle of its forehead from your penis—get over it. The baby is sealed in the fluid cocoon of the uterus, floating peacefully until it is time to make its arrival. The act of sex, the rocking motion, is probably comforting for the baby. Second, unless your doctor has ruled sex off limits for medical reasons, sex during pregnancy is healthy for Mom, the baby, and the health of your relation-ship. Studies have shown that couples who remain intimate during pregnancy when permitted have a higher rate of staying sexual after the birth of the baby. How's that for a great incentive for keeping it sexy during pregnancy!

The hormones produced during sex (our old friend oxytocin) bond Mommy to you and the baby, and these hormones can pass through the placental barrier; so, in theory, this extra dose of oxytocin may even help the baby, creating more oxytocin receptors as the brain develops. Couples who remain sexually active during pregnancy have lower rates of premature labor in comparison to those who abstain. Your woman may want sex and a lot of it. All those hormones in massive doses floating through her bloodstream usually increase her libido, and many women can't get enough! There is also an amazing sense of freedom. You are already pregnant, so preventing preg-nancy is not an issue. Spontaneity rules! Take advantage of this time, especially during the second trimester, before sex can become uncomfortable as the baby grows ex-ponentially in her belly. Be sure to focus on her orgasm; it will make her hungry for more!

While a woman is pregnant, all those hormones in her body have brought about a few physiological changes you may not be aware of. Her nerve endings are on fire; she tingles all over because she is also carrying around about fifty percent more blood than usual. That blood flows everywhere, especially into her genitals, so her vulva, labia, clitoris, and breasts are engorged and probably look different too. She is turned on a lot of the time because her body is so sensitive, her lubrication levels are high, and she is almost guaranteed to be multiorgasmic. For some women, pregnancy is the first time they get to experience being multiorgasmic. (Of course, *your* woman has already experienced that...you are a Love Warrior!) Her skin craves your touch, and not just sexually. Touch her a lot because, as her pregnancy progresses, the more you touch her, the better she will feel emotionally and physically. Her entire body is being stretched and pulled in new and different ways. Her feet and hands will swell from all the water and blood she's carrying, and everything is sore. Massage is a vital part of keeping your pregnant partner happy, so do it often. It will also keep her feeling loved and sexy and wanting you, so it's a win-win for everyone!

While you are pregnant, sexual intimacy will take on a new meaning in your relationship. This is a magical time to deepen your understanding of love, when you realize that love is what brought you to this place. Rejoice in that love and the creation of a new life, again through sex. Of course, that is all profound, but the most important thing to remember is this: maintain a sense of humor! Sex during pregnancy can be challenging as her body changes, but it is more than feasible. Sexual positions you can use will change as she does, and the most important thing is to listen to your partner and for her to listen to her body. If something doesn't feel good, stop and try something else. Just don't stop trying!

Let's chat about positions and what works best. By her 4th month, your proud mama will no longer be allowed to lie on her back for sex, or sleep for that matter. (Lying on her back puts too much pressure on major blood vessels that feed the baby. You don't want to be on top of her by this point either—too much pressure on her belly.) The best position at this stage of her pregnancy is Woman on Top – she has total control of how much penetration she has, and either you or she can stimulate her clitoris and her breasts. You can also rub her tummy gently, which will make you both feel bonded to the baby. A variation on this position, reverse cowgirl, where she is on top and facing away from you, is great too. She can still control how much of you is inside her, either one of you can stimulate other parts of her body, and the direction of your penis is different, which will give her a little variety in sensation from penetration. Remember, all of her genitals are extra sensitive, so those pleasure points inside the vagina, the G, X and Y spots, are all going to feel amazing!

As she gets larger through her second and into her third trimester, you will probably have to readjust sex positions. The baby is now somewhat in the way, so positions where her belly can hang free are best. The most popular is rear entry, or doggy style. Be sure to prop her up on a lot of pillows so she's comfortable. From this position, she can stimulate her clitoris by hand or using a vibrator, if you can't reach or if you're busy holding yourself up! At this point, it's hard to have intercourse in a position where you can also look at each other or kiss, so be sure to do a lot of kissing and eye contact before and after intercourse. A variation of the rear entry position is lying side to side and entering her from behind. This is great if she is low on strength, since she doesn't have to hold herself up. Experiment with what works for you, and continue to have sex as long as she is comfortable and willing.

When intercourse becomes too cumbersome or when she is feeling sexual but not in the mood for penetration, rely on oral sex. The beauty of oral sex is that it's a great way to help her climax repeatedly, especially when her libido is high. If she also wants penetration, you can use your fingers and hands if intercourse isn't in the cards. Remember, her orgasm is important—she and the baby get all the hormonal benefits of sex, and you get to be her Love Warrior hero! Who knows, she may want to return the oral favor!

Esther: Historically, midwives have always recommended orgasm for pregnant women, especially during labor. While many Western women have experienced episiotomies, where the skin and sometimes vital muscles get cut to allow safe passage for the baby and to avoid tearing, many non-Western women have tried a different approach. Midwives have invited husbands into the labor room, excused themselves, and asked the male partner to bring his wife to orgasm. The hormones released will relax the muscles of the pelvis and vagina, and, in many cases, eliminate the need for the episiotomy. Another great reason to climax!

Stay flexible and enjoy this time!

Some things are going to be different. As we mentioned, her lubrication levels will be high, so keep some towels under the bed so nobody has to sleep in the wet spot. Her breasts are big, inviting, and they may leak breast milk during sex. Don't freak out—it's normal and should be expected, especially later in the pregnancy. She's going to get uncomfortable. Sleep will be difficult, since she can only lie on her side, and she has to be propped up everywhere with pillows to cushion her and the baby. Be cognizant of these changes and try to help. Soft music or the sounds of the ocean may help her sleep—go find some. She is going to be tired all the time, so be prepared to take over some of her household chores, especially cooking, cleaning, and caring for any other children in the house. She is still going to be emotional, and she needs constant reassurance that you still find her beautiful and sexy. TELL HER! Shower her with compliments, romantic musings, love notes, sexy gifts like lingerie or massage oils, and help her use them. Be sure you are her true hero. Be prepared to run out at 3:00 a.m. to fetch ice cream for her cravings, to rub her feet when she can't possibly walk another step, to polish her toenails or shave her legs for her because she can't reach anymore, and to take her out and show her off at a nice restaurant or dancing if she's game. Rejoice in this experience and show her how much fun you're having. She will love you for it.

Remember to take good care of yourself too. Eating healthy, for all of you, is incredibly important and will be easy to control if you take over the meal preparations. You may want to start exercising regularly if you don't already, since you are going to need your strength for extra chores, and more upper body strength to take charge of sexual positions later in the pregnancy. (We'll bet that's the best reason you ever heard for doing pushups!) Go for daily walks with mom-to-be; it's great for both of you and the baby, and it will help keep her swelling down. Stay involved—go to all of her doctor's appointments with her, go to the birthing classes, and practice the birthing techniques at home. This adventure changes daily, so don't miss any part of it, and watch how your relationship becomes stronger and more passionate with each passing day!

We understand that this may sound really overwhelming to many men. If this sounds like you will be working a second job, career by day and dad-to-be by night, you are. She is working two jobs full time, 24 hours a day, as the mother of your unborn child and that is no small task, physically and emotionally, and possibly working her job during the day, or caring for your other children. We are encouraging you to be her hero. While it may be difficult to make the time to go with her to every doctor's appointment or to take over all of her household responsibilities in addition to your own, please help her and join her in as much as you can since she has very little choice in the matter. She has to leave her job and go to the doctor, with or without you. Be her Love Warrior—go with her, support her, and be her rock. Studies show that the more involved you are in your pregnancy, the closer the two of you will be once the baby arrives, and the healthier the baby will be too. This is a family affair!

Love Her Right

Pregnancy is an incredible time for you both, and the magic of this period will never happen again, especially since each pregnancy is different. As you prepare for the joys and challenges of parenthood, one of the most important things to remember is that this family you are creating started with the two of you...with a love that has created life. Encourage romance and passion during this time, and they will follow you throughout your life together. Nurture that love the same way you are planning to nurture that child, and the strength and power of that love will carry you through all of life's challenges. From our hearts to yours: Mazel Tov!

CHAPTER 21.

Menstruation to Menopause:
How To Be Her Hero During Her Difficult Times

Every twenty-eight or so days your woman gets her period. We can't for the life of us to figure out why some women call it their "friend." You are nobody's friend when you are bitchy, bloated, and you feel like your uterus has been kicked by a horse. Imagine if you were getting kicked in the balls for a week. Then, women bleed like hell, and you can't touch their breasts, which hurt even if you're just **looking** at them. (This should be all the time if you are a typical guy!)

Here's the game plan on how to deal with her during her hormonal cycle. Again, no one can foretell, even her, how painful or strong her symptoms may be because one of her ovaries has just spit out an egg, her uterus was filled with blood-soaked tissue—just in case you were looking to have a baby—and now her uterus is letting go of the uterine tissue and blood because she isn't pregnant. Having sex during her period is sometimes a turnoff to a guy.

It may surprise you that if you ask a woman about sex and her period, some will tell you that they are really horny during different times of the menstrual cycle. You just have to ask her what does or does not feel good. Don't let it get you frustrated if she tells you that her nipples are too sore to touch. You can try to circle all around the nipple area, or try using the BACK of your hand. Don't squeeze her breast hard; instead, gently cup her breasts and softly rub her over her chest plate, between her breasts and her stomach and her sides as you make your way down her body. Plant lots of soft kisses on those spots. If you have soft hair on your face, softly rub your cheeks over her skin. Shower her with kisses on her neck, the sides of her face, eyelids, and explore her mouth with yours. Tell her how beautiful she is and reinforce how much you love making love with her. Make her feel like a goddess, and tell her how grateful you are to be able to pleasure her.

What if you want to make love and she's bleeding? Keep some dark towels under the bed. No one will feel awkward from having wrecked the sheets and having to look at a little blood. So you might have a little bloodlike stuff on your penis. It will wash off, not a big deal. Just remember that you squirt too, and a towel will keep one of you from having to sleep in the wet spot.

Try different positions to see which is more comfortable for her. Sometimes when a woman is on top, she can control how much of you enters her. Her uterus is much larger than usual; if your penis is ramming against her cervix or uterus, it can be uncomfortable or downright painful for her. Also, when she is on top, you or she can play with her clitoris at the same time that you're inside her for extra squeezing on you and more fun for her and her hungry clitoris! Watching a woman play with herself while she is on top is a mad turn-on to watch from below. She needs to feel safe and secure enough to play with herself in front of you, so softly encourage her and enjoy the show. You can try making love on your sides. Then, your body weight is not on top of her swollen belly, which takes away from her having her share of the fun. This also frees up your hands to wander, play, or run your fingers through her hair while she moans in ecstasy.

If you are wondering if you can have oral sex with her during her period...of course you can! Only **you** can decide if this doesn't turn you on, just like some women don't like giving blow jobs all of the time. Remember to be creative and do what feels good mentally and physically for you both. Know that menstrual blood doesn't have cooties or germs and won't harm you. It may only get on your face. She can also put a tampon in her vagina during oral sex, so you don't have to deal with menstrual blood. She may LOVE receiving oral sex during her period.

Now, we are going to fast forward to the next major hurdle in a women's sexual existence: menopause.

Menopause is a tough time for all involved. Most guys would probably rename it as "Man On Pause" because of her lack of libido. This is the time in a woman's life when she stops menstruating. It can start slowly by her missing some periods until ultimately they stop altogether. During this transition, many women feel less sexual, due to lower estrogen levels. Every woman has different symptoms including insomnia, hot flashes, weight gain, vaginal dryness, and OH NO…MOOD SWINGS. Sometimes she probably wants to peel off her skin; sometimes it seems to have a mind of its own. You need to ask her what her body is going through, so you can figure out how to work around these changes and find a dance that works for both of you.

To get your partner interested in sex again, our first suggestion is to court her all over again. Remind her how sexy you find her; make her feel beautiful—that can never hurt. With the wild hormone fluctuations and decreasing levels of estrogen in her body, she may not be feeling sexy or pretty; additionally, she may be feeling like she is losing her mind. But, you can stimulate her brain with romance to produce more oxytocin, which will increase her libido! Sometimes a woman has hot flashes, so she sweats a lot, and you may have to make sure that the temperature in the room is comfortable.

The next frustrating part of menopause is vaginal dryness. Compound this with the thinning of the vaginal walls, caused by the sudden drop in her estrogen levels, and you have The Perfect Storm for making sex feel lousy. Trust us...penetration without enough lubrication just HURTS! Your partner is just as frustrated because she feels like she doesn't own her body anymore, and it isn't working like it used to. Just like if you can't get it up...you just don't feel manly, right? Since she may have decreased vaginal secretions, try to keep some water-based lubricant near the bedside. Vitamin E vaginal suppositories used twice weekly can help enormously. All of these situations are normal, and one just has to be loving and gentle to let her know that you want to work through it.

The next issue is her lack of ability to feel as much because the skin inside the vagina thins and the nerves are not as sensitive. You probably think that you need to scream right now, but don't give up. We have the answers for all of these inevitable issues. Every woman WILL go through menopause. But, we are Love Warriors and we love a challenge! Step up to the challenge and we'll give you the insider's tips on how to fix it!

Steps to dealing with menopause

Step 1. Talk to her more.

Our biggest sexual organ is between our ears. What we hear, we understand. What we don't hear, we fill in the blanks for lack of other information. Compliment her more! We all want to feel better about ourselves. For example: "You look really great tonight," "Those colors look really sexy on you," and "Your shoes are really hot." A woman loves that you notice her shoes, hair, jewelry, or just that you notice HER for the details that she puts into her looks. She needs to HEAR the words. Who doesn't like a compliment?

Esther: For those of us who are insecure on a good day, hormonal fluctuations only magnify our insecurities. Nothing makes me feel sexier than when Joni notices a change in my hair or a sexy new pair of shoes. Try out a compliment with sexual innuendo and see what happens to your little vixen!

Step 2. Use foods that can help deal with lack of libido.

Different foods and beverages can ignite her fire before you ever step foot in the bedroom. Start with the aphrodisiac section in this book to learn more about this ancient science. Eat and get eaten! Yahoo!

Step 3. Try supplements to build up her libido.

We are currently researching daily supplements that may help build libido in women, especially while going through menopause. For now, the other choices are hormone replacement therapy, which would involve a physician to check her hormone levels, although many women cannot take hormones because it dramatically increases their risks for estrogenic cancers. (Unfortunately, studies are now showing that HRT treatments like Premarin and Prempro actually *contribute* to vaginal thinning and dryness. The problems may take six to twelve months to develop after stopping the drugs. Some doctors believe it's because of the strong horse estrogens they contain.) There are also many prescription estrogen products that can be applied vaginally. Compounding pharmacies make the most natural ones, such as low-dose estriol vaginal cream. Vaginal application of these low-dose estrogens does not appear to carry the health risks of synthetic HRT that is taken orally. There are also natural women's supplements that can be found at your local drug store or natural food stores. One is called black cohosh, and there are also capsules that are combinations of herbs and vitamins to specifically relieve her symptoms. Wild Yam is a cream that has testosterone-like properties. Always check with a physician to make sure that the herbs do not conflict with any other medications that she may be taking.

Step 4. Get her in the mood.

Start a seduction with a warm massage or bath to help her relax. Stress will reduce her ability to get turned on too, so help her get through it. Or, give her a long, naked massage, starting with her lying down, so that you start with her back. Use lots of massage oil and keep talking to her and telling her how beautiful her body is. Don't listen to her self-criticisms, because she may be feeling crappy about her body. Just use your hands and lovingly caress her body. Take some time and go a little deeper into her shoulders and down the middle of her spine. Use the massage oil down her buttocks and down the back of her legs, and massage the back of her calves. Women who wear heels are tight in their lower leg area. She should start to relax. If she starts to rub her body back toward you, rub her with your whole body. Kiss the back of her neck and shoulders. Let the fun begin after that!

Step 5. Help to increase her sensitivity and lubrication.

Now we need to add some external lubrication to help when you decide that it is time to stimulate her genitals. We suggest using water-based lubricants, not the same massage oil that you were using before. Check out the Intimate Organics line of products at our store site. They make a light water-based lubricant called **Hydra** that is close to her natural pH balance. They also make an external gel that may intensify her orgasms if she is having decreased sensitivity in her clitoris. Try the **Intimate Organic Intense Clitoral Gel.** It's certified organic and contains two amino acids that stimulate blood flow to the clitoris. It's one of our favorites! **Intimate Organics** also has the **Discover G-Spot Gel** for helping you find her G-Spot by making it swell; once you find it, you will set her off into orgasmic fireworks. There are also some other brands of fun, flavored lubes so that she can taste like strawberries, cotton candy, etc. Again, the more foreplay you give her, the more turned on she will be. Use a lot of tongue play to add extra lubrication, insert a few fingers into her, and slowly start to arouse her. Again, please be sure she is fully aroused (really wet—remember our rule: she comes first!) before you proceed to intercourse to be sure of minimizing any discomfort.

Step 6. Getting ready for intercourse.

After her first orgasm, put some lube on your penis and slide in slowly, letting her open up at her speed until you are fully inside her. Once you are fully in her, **pause** for a second and look into her eyes for the go-ahead sign, and slowly start to pull out and in. Starting softly first is always better until she can tell you to do her harder. Then, you and she can watch each other's body language to gauge speed and how hard to go. When in doubt, ask her, "How can I give you the most pleasure?" Keep asking her and get direct answers, or keep teasing her with your mouth and hands until she begs for more!

Step 7. Other ways to make her feel sexy and sexual.

If you are feeling adventurous, try surprising her with a new sexy piece of lingerie—for you! Candles and sexy music will add to the mood, and you want to do everything that you can to start to get her in the mood. Give her a lap dance and maybe a massage to get her in the mood as a start of foreplay. Maybe a little striptease from you is all it takes! A little something sexy for her, like a new piece of lingerie, will help her realize how sexy you think she is. She's lucky to have a guy that is thoughtful enough to seek out a solution to a frustrating time! Remember that the female brain always wants romance before sex, so keep up the romantic side of your relationship to feed her brain with romantic and sexy thoughts to get and keep her in the mood.

Step 8. Quit Taking Everything Personally and Remember to have fun!

Sex and romance are about more than two bodies rubbing together. When her hormones get the best of her, remember this acronym: **QTIP—Quit Taking It Personally**! Sometimes her moodiness is beyond her control, so just let it roll off your back. Go with the flow, and change tactics if you need to. Sometimes, laughter is the best medicine, so take yourselves less seriously and enjoy the journey. True love is all about weathering the tough times and celebrating the best of times...and sex is all about the best of times!

Life is filled with body changes. Every time something is different for one of you, it is your job, as a couple, to talk about it and figure out how to make it work for both of you. There are no obstacles, only opportunities to keep your sex life hot and passionate at each turn in the road. There will always be turns in the road of life. As Love Warriors, you have what it takes to conquer any of them if you really want it. We know that you can!

CHAPTER 22.

Straight Talk For Him: Erectile Dysfunction, Low T, And The Unreliable Mr. Willie

We know you don't want to talk about getting older and the changes that our bodies go through. While it's common for women (in our culture that is obsessed with youth and nimble bodies that have yet to experience the effects of gravity) to hate discussing aging and its torrid effects, it is becoming as common for men to run quietly from the room when the age conversation rears its balding head. Well, we're here together to discuss the tough topics, and this one isn't going to get swept under the rug, so hold onto your golf clubs and let go of your misconceptions, because in this case: the truth will not only set you free, it may also save your life.

Time Marches On—But You Can Determine the Beat!

As we age, we can see physical changes in our bodies. For men, hair will start growing in places it doesn't belong and stop growing where you actually want it. Sports become tougher to play, every part of your body makes noise when you move, and recovery time after a wild night on the town is longer than the actual night on the town. When it comes time for romance, sometimes Mr. Willie isn't standing at full attention or he's just plain uninterested. What the hell is happening?

Here's the truth. Changes are going to happen. How drastic those changes are will depend on several factors:

- How well you've taken care of yourself so far
- Your current lifestyle
- Your genetic makeup

Some things you can't do anything about. If baldness runs in your family, get ready to shave your head one day and go for the sexy, bald look. If other members of your family have experienced cardiovascular disease, cancer, diabetes, or high blood pressure, you may be genetically predisposed to these conditions. **That DOES NOT MEAN that you are destined to get any of these conditions.** It just means that you may want to be more purposeful in your lifestyle choices than men without these family histories. Whether you deteriorate physically as you age is largely up to you.

Let's take a physical inventory: Are you currently suffering from high blood pressure, diabetes, cardiovascular disease, or obesity? If the answer to any of these is yes, or if you are currently considered prediabetic, meaning your sugar levels in your bloodstream are above normal (over a score of 110 on a fasting glucose blood test but below 126), you are possibly already experiencing difficulties getting and/or sustaining an erection. Erectile Dysfunction (ED) is a symptom of these conditions, and it is also a side effect of the medications you might be taking, especially in the case of high blood pressure and diabetes. **(If you don't know the answer to any of these questions—DO NOT PASS GO, DO NOT COLLECT $200—GO DIRECTLY TO YOUR DOCTOR FOR A PHYSICAL! Not knowing or avoiding knowing about your health is no excuse!)**

What ED Is and Why You Should Be Concerned

Erectile Dysfunction is defined as having difficulty achieving and maintaining an erection 50 percent of the time. What that means is that if Mr. Willie isn't in the mood once in a while, or after you've had too good a time with alcohol or drugs involved, that's normal. If you start to feel that Mr. Willie is on vacation without you, or that he's on his own schedule that you don't have access to, that's a more significant problem. Why? Well, because ED, that 50 percent of the time kind, can be an indicator of much more serious health problems. We'll bet that you didn't know that **as of 2006, the American Medical Association mandated that all erectile dysfunction patients with no other cardiac symptoms are to be treated and categorized as heart patients until proven otherwise**. According to Randy Fagin, urologist and director of the Prostate Center of Austin, Texas, "ED is quite literally vascular disease under the belt." The arteries in the penis are one quarter of the diameter of the arteries in your heart, so when plaque builds up, the slender vessels feel strangulation first, but cardiac problems are often around the corner. Cardiologists predict that ED occurs 3-4 years before traditional cardiac symptoms do such as chest pain or a heart attack. ED has become known as the best warning sign for a possible future cardiac event. **More than one-third of men over forty experience unreliable erections, so if you're one of them, SEE YOUR DOCTOR!**

There are also a host of medical conditions that can be behind erectile dysfunction. Let's look at a few of them, so you can figure out if this problem is in your pants and not just in your head.

1. Diabetes: Diabetes can cause nerve and artery damage that can make achieving an erection difficult. According the National Institutes of Health, between 35 percent and 50 percent of men with diabetes experience ED. Some estimates are higher, stating that up to 75 percent of men with diabetes will experience at least some degree of ED during their lifetime, and the risk increases with age. Controlling your diabetes with medication and/or consistent and significant changes in your diet and exercise level will stabilize your sugar levels and may help your ED symptoms—another good reason to get in shape and put down the junk food!

2. Kidney disease: Kidney disease can cause chemical changes to occur in your body that affect circulation, hormones, energy level, and nerve function. Sometimes these changes will lower a person's libido (sex drive) or sexual ability. Drugs used to treat kidney disease may also cause ED.

3. Neurological (nerve and brain) diseases: The nervous system plays a vital part in achieving and maintaining an erection, and it is common for men with diseases such as stroke, multiple sclerosis (MS), Alzheimer's disease, Parkinson's disease, and spinal cord injuries to experience ED. This is due to an interruption in the transmission of nerve impulses between the brain and the penis.

4. Vascular disease: Vascular diseases are those that affect the blood vessels. These diseases include atherosclerosis (hardening of the arteries), hypertension, and high cholesterol. As we discussed above, these diseases, which account for 70 percent of physically related causes of ED, all restrict blood flow to the heart, the brain, and, in the case of ED, the penis.

5. Prostate Cancer: Prostate cancer doesn't cause ED on its own, but treatment (radiation, hormonal manipulation, or surgery to remove the cancer) can lead to erectile problems.

Diseases are not the only culprits when it comes to ED. There are other causes:

1. Surgery: Surgery performed to treat diseases such as prostate cancer and bladder cancer often require the removal of nerves and tissues around the affected area, which can lead to ED. Some of these surgeries result in only temporary problems (lasting six to eighteen months) while others result in permanent damage to the nerves and tissue around the penis and require treatment in order for an erection to be achieved.
2. Injury: Injuries to the pelvis, bladder, spinal cord, and penis that require surgery also commonly cause ED.
3. Hormonal Imbalances: Imbalances of hormones, such as thyroid hormones, prolactin, and testosterone can affect a man's response to sexual stimulation. These imbalances can be the result of a tumor of the pituitary gland, kidney disease, liver disease, or hormonal treatment of prostate cancer.
4. Venous leak: If the veins in the penis allow blood to leave the penis during an erection, an erection cannot be maintained. This is known as a venous leak and can be a result of injury or disease.
5. Tobacco, alcohol, or drug use: All three of these substances can damage a person's blood vessels permanently and/or restrict blood flow to the penis, causing ED. **Smoking in particular plays a large role in causing ED in people with arteriosclerosis. Smoking is one of the primary causes of arterial constriction related ED.**

6. Prostate enlargement: Bladder neck obstruction due to prostate enlargement has recently been associated with varying degrees of ED. Get your prostate checked regularly by your doctor—bend over, turn your head, and cough, my friend!
7. In addition to these conditions, there are over 200 types of prescription medications that can cause ED.

The bottom line is this: erectile dysfunction is not a normal condition associated with aging; it is a warning sign that something may be seriously wrong elsewhere in your body. **If you are experiencing any erectile problems more often than once in a while, GO TO THE DOCTOR. No one likes the doctor, and no one wants to talk about these kinds of issues, go Do It Anyway! Your life might depend on it.**

Here's the biggest problem with ED—the treatments. Viagra, Cialis, Levitra, and this whole class of drugs can help you get Mr. Willie back to playing on your schedule, but at a cost. The side effects, which are significantly more common than the commercials mention (over one-third of users suffer from them), are serious and unpleasant, and include headaches, heartburn, vision problems, or prolonged, painful erections. (In rare cases even blindness!) Viagra is NOT an aphrodisiac, and it won't make you bigger. It's also proven to be physically addictive, so if you abuse it, you may have permanent problems achieving a normal erection without it. It also won't make your erection any better if ED isn't your problem, so don't try popping a little blue pill if you're under a lot of stress or too drunk to perform—it won't help. Viagra is not a recreational drug!

Low T and Andropause

Unless you've been living under a rock, you probably know that women go through a hormonal transition in their fifties called menopause, where their periods eventually stop coming and their ovaries stop producing eggs. They also experience symptoms for what can be years of declining hormone levels until the transition is complete and the body restabilizes. (Our symptoms tend to be more dramatic because the hormone levels, toward the end of menopause, decline quickly.) What you may not know is that both men and women experience this age-related decline in hormones, and the effects can be surprisingly similar.

In men, this condition is sometimes referred to as andropause, and the most significant hormonal decline is in testosterone levels. Andropause is different, since the decline in testosterone happens over a long period of time, starting in your thirties, so the symptoms you may feel are a slow but noticeable increase over decades. It's after about age forty-five that this decline in testosterone becomes particularly noticeable in some men and where treatment may be warranted. Today's medical industry is currently referring to this condition as Low Testosterone, or Low T for short. Low T is different from ED because the symptoms are more widespread than just problems with Mr. Willie. In addition to Willie's lack of enthusiasm, Low T sufferers also experience fatigue, depression, decline in athletic ability, decrease in lean muscle mass, possible weight gain, decrease in bone density, and decreased libido. Sound familiar? These are all symptoms that women experience during menopause. Currently, there are an estimated 13 million men suffering from Low T, but only about 10 percent are being treated for it. If these symptoms sound familiar or if your partner says these are symptoms you've been exhibiting, go get simple blood tests to measure your testosterone levels.

The tests you need are:

1. Free Testosterone
2. Prolactin

3. SHBG (sex hormone binding globulin)
4. Total testosterone

*Tell your doctor you want all four tests, no matter what the doctor says! It's the comparison of all these levels that diagnoses Low T.

Low testosterone levels are associated with obesity, diabetes, depression, and possibly cardiovascular disease, and may serve as a marker of health decline in general. Testosterone is used by the body to build bones, and Low T can lead to osteoporosis (thinning of the bones)—men with hip fractures tend to have low testosterone levels. If you are experiencing Low T, there is a topical bio-identical hormone treatment gel that is easy to use. Within thirty days, your symptoms will dissipate. If you follow treatment for a longer period, your symptoms should vanish.

What You Can Do To Help Mr. Willie and Your Heart Stay Healthy

If you already suffer from ED, Low T, or diabetes, high blood pressure, cardiovascular disease, or obesity, or if you are worried because Mr. Willie has been acting up lately (or not, as the case may be), the steps to fixing this state of affairs are simple and doable. They take commitment to your health and well-being for yourself and your relationship. You want to be around to dance at your granddaughter's wedding, don't you? Then do something about it.

- **Use it or lose it.** Stay in peak performance as long as possible. A University of Chicago study proved that good health promotes good sex, and good sex promotes good health! That means have sex and have it often—it's good for you and your partner as you age gracefully.

- **Maintain a healthy body weight by exercising and following a diet of whole grains, lean proteins, fruits, and lots of green veggies.** Fruits and vegetables have a lot of antioxidants, and amazing things happen to our bodies when we provide the nutrients we need for the body to heal itself. If you don't exercise regularly, start now. If you work a job where you sit a lot and have never been a big fan of exercise, like us, start incorporating subtle exercise into your lifestyle. Go for a walk after dinner with your honey and hold hands while you walk the dog...take the kids too. Fresh air never killed anyone. Are you near a beach or a state park? Go enjoy it with your loved ones. Buy a pedometer (a step counter—an under $20 investment), clip it to your waistband, and walk—take the stairs, park a little farther from work than usual, and count your steps from morning to night. Your first goal is 10,000 steps per day. After you can consistently do that, work up to 15,000 steps per day. It's not easy, but the benefits will be startling. You will trim down, have more energy, and probably experience an increase in sex drive—we know you'll hate that! (The good news is your partner will be feeling the same great results, so it's time to party!) **A 2004 study of obese men with ED found that a third of the men who improved their overall conditions through diet and exercise and lost an average of 30 lbs improved their ED conditions without medication.**

Dr. Joni: We know that many men worry about their penis size... is it enough to please her? You will be happy to know that when you lose a significant amount of belly fat, you and your partner are closer during sex, and you will see that your belly was getting in the way, which gave you performance doubts. The size of Mr. Willie was just right!

- **Quit smoking right now!** Smoking is the primary reason for arterial constriction ED. The chemicals also wreak havoc on your hormonal system and throw off your levels, which can affect your sex drive. If cigarette packs had a surgeon general's warning: "Smoking can lead to lack of erections," every man on the planet would quit immediately! Do yourself a favor and quit, and get your friends to quit too. Would you rather smoke or have sex? You choose.

- **Reduce your stress levels.** Stress can kill, and you don't need us to tell you that. It can also kill your sex life. The stress hormone cortisol is a sex drive destroyer because it sucks up all the good hormones that make you want sex and feel sexy. We're not telling you to go sit at the top of a mountain and contemplate the meaning of life, but if that appeals to you, go for it. At a minimum, commit to spending at least ten minutes a day in silence: no cell phone, no e-mail, no coworkers, no interruptions. Just sit, and allow your mind to be still—it will add years to your life. Cutting back on your stress will do more than increase the duration of your life, it will also magnify the quality of your life. Reducing stress will make you happier, and it will increase your sex drive. Happy people want to get laid, which goes for both of you. Work as a team with your partner and help each other lower your individual stress levels so you can come together (figuratively and literally) on a deeper level, as often as possible. Creating a simple division of chores, as we discussed earlier, is a great place to start relieving each other of stress. Try giving each other massages or foot rubs—massage is the number one way to reduce stress on a purely physical level.

Esther: I can speak volumes about stress. Stress affects everything, from my energy levels to my food choices to my sex drive. I have had to make some radical changes in my diet and exercise habits to deal with stress, and I have experienced what happens when you let stress take a toll on your health and relationship. Don't let any job or any source of stress become a drain on your sex life or on your relationship. Nothing is more important to me than the health and well-being of my passionate marriage. Make that same declaration, and you will stop allowing anyone else to dictate what's important in your life. Stand up for your right to be happy, and your life will transform before your eyes—and so will the quality of your sex life. Yippee!

🔥 **Strive for regular sleep patterns.** If you can get eight hours of sleep a night, do it. The exercise you're adding to your daily routine, and reducing your stress level, will also help you sleep better, as will your increased libido (and your hotter sex life!). Quality sleep gives your body the chance to heal itself and allows cells to regenerate, so it's vital to long-term good health. Cut back on the alcohol, sugar, and caffeine, since they are central nervous system stimulants and can impair your ability to have sweet dreams. If you snore, have your doctor check you for sleep apnea, which is when your brain doesn't get enough oxygen while you are sleeping. Losing weight may also help reduce sleep apnea. Your brain needs oxygen to function, and you are not getting quality sleep without oxygen. Your partner will sleep better too!

Why You Want to Stay Sexually Active (other than the obvious reasons!)

According to a British Medical Journal, 57 percent of men and 52 percent of women in their seventies are enjoying regular sex. A University of Chicago Study said 25 percent of seventy-five- to eighty-five-year-olds are sexually active. While this might have something to do with the Viagra phenomenon, the reality is that we can all have healthy, vibrant sex lives until the Grim Reaper comes knocking. There are many reasons to keep heating up the sheets, other than the fact that it feels so great (if you're doing it right—the fact that you're reading this book ensures that you are!). Staying sexually active gives us feelings of joy, excitement, and connectedness with another person, hopefully your soul mate. Physiologically, regular sex also boosts the immune system and releases hormones that lower stress levels and improve sleep. An active sex life might even hold off the aging process. A Scottish study found that people who enjoy sex every other day look 7-12 years younger than their sexually inactive peers. (Tell your wife to save the money and forget the Botox—turn off the TV and have some fun instead and look great naturally. Watch how fast she starts peeling her clothes off!)

The point is that no matter where you are right now, no matter what state your health is in now, or how much you weigh, you can make simple changes in your diet and daily activities to alter your future health. Keep it sexy and real—the long-term success of any relationship is the ability of both partners to be 100 percent responsible for their own lives and their own health as well as 100 percent responsible for the health of your relationship. If you're healthy right now, great, stay that way. If your physical condition could use some improvement (or a complete overhaul) then make the commitment to yourself and to your partner to do things differently. Keep life fun and sexy. Enjoy each other, and keep striving to live your lives more passionately so every day is a new sexy adventure you can look forward to, no matter how old you are. Remember that you will have great stories to reminisce about as you age sexually together!

Esther: Look, I'm no hypocrite. As I'm writing this section, I'm currently about 25 lbs overweight, and I'm experiencing some of the symptoms we've discussed in this chapter. Having just turned forty, I will admit that I'm taking a new approach to my lifelong struggle with my weight. Along with changing my eating habits, I have made a commitment to do something physically challenging every day. For me, that means ninety minutes of Hot Yoga, a thirty-minute strength training DVD and striving for the elusive ten thousand steps a day. Remember, I have always HATED exercise, and I detest not eating whatever I want—I love food. But, I love Joni more, and I don't want to miss one extra day with her because I chose a pastrami sandwich over a salad. I would rather forgo the sandwich, and enact a sexual fantasy with Joni any day. I know all the diet and lifestyle gurus say you have to lose weight for yourself, and I agree. For me, my desire to have as much time on this Earth with my partner is completely and wholeheartedly selfish, and that time is something I'm willing to fight for and sacrifice for. So I'll sweat and huff and puff and curse a little and grumble a lot when I make the food choices I should, instead of what I want, because I know what my reward is, and it doesn't get any better than that! That's OK. She's worth it!

CHAPTER 23.
Maintaining Intimacy Through Illnesses and Major Bumps In The Road

Why do we want to talk about what seems like a real mood killer of a conversation? That is precisely why we want to address this tough reality. As life progresses, all relationships will have major bumps in the road from menopause and ED to cancer and other life-threatening diseases. They may affect you, your partner, a friend, or loved one. Regardless, they ultimately put a heavy stress upon your relationship.

Some of the more major issues may last longer than others, but you need tools to handle these situations because life gives no guarantees that all will remain perfect forever. Both the ill person and the caretaker experience different levels of fear, abandonment, loneliness, and even anger as they deal with these tough times. All of this is completely normal and justified, and some of these issues need to be aired via conversation with your partner or with the aid of a therapist in order to keep your sanity and maintain the romance and sex in your relationship as much as possible.

The word "romance" is where the emotions of love exist. So how can romance exist in the face of tragedy? Can you or your partner handle the world of changes that were thrown upon you, or will one of you walk out or stop loving the other? Perhaps you need to examine your ability to handle fear. We all live with certain fears in life...

fear of abandonment, fear of losing the love of your life, fear of being alone, and fear of dying. Fear can drive a wedge between you and your partner, even though these feelings are appropriate and normal. It can lead to your drifting apart on certain levels and can lead to the next level, which is anger.

Anger can come from the ill person or the caretaker or both. The ill person is asking him or herself, "Why me?" The well person is angry too. The well person may have survivor guilt and even question God as to why he or she has to deal with this illness that has totally disrupted life. You may feel out of control and helpless. Sometimes, the well partner has so much fear and anger that he or she shuts down and backs away from the ill person because of an inability to handle the reality of watching a loved one suffer; that reaction is based on his or her own inner fears.

People don't know how they will handle these life issues unless they have experienced them before, but each time seems to be difficult, and it will depend on the strength of your relationship and your own inner strength whether you will allow the illness to own your life or you will rise up to the challenge and make the best of what you can control and conquer your fears and anger.

Dr. Joni: My grandmother was a caretaker for my grandfather for most of my life. He became wheelchair bound, and I knew that they were no longer intimate. But, every day, she bathed him, fed him, nursed his bed sores, and lifted him into bed with a hydraulic lift. He was over 6' tall and she was maybe 5'2." This went on for over fifty years. I asked her one day how she managed to do this day after day. Her response was simply, "When life gives you lemons, you need to learn to make lemonade." I now live by this credo. It came in handy when I had to face my mother's battle with breast cancer and again when a previous partner got diagnosed with advanced breast cancer at age 38. I thought that, as a doctor, I could heal anyone, but even the strongest of us struggle under the additional weight of dealing with having to be strong for someone else and not having anyone to hold you up. I read every self-help book and studied macrobiotic diets that are known to have curative powers. I also had the additional pressure of maintaining my dental practice at the same time without it appearing that I was under extreme stress.

I chose to control what I could and let the rest be handled by more supreme powers. It sounds a lot easier than it was. So, I cooked healing foods and made sure that I stayed strong because I had to survive, even if she may not. I was blessed that they both survived and are alive today. I can only hope that my positive energy and spirit inspired them to fight too.

Although the relationship with my partner did not last after all of the healing was over, it was not for lack of my trying. I have no regrets and realized that the relationship had problems long before cancer came into the picture, and we parted as friends. I still wish her all of the love that she deserves, as I have found all of the love that I deserve in my Esther.

We have seen couples who allow their anger to be reflected upon the caretaker and vice versa. This leads to a miserable, negative relationship, but it is common for the ill person to try to push the caretaker away, or for the caretaker to resent the ill person for having changed their lives. The caretaker is now solely responsible for handling all of the household chores, continuing to work, caring for the kids, and still maintaining your sanity. We understand that you may be grieving the loss of the life that you had... the one that you wanted and was taken away from you. When in doubt, please talk to a therapist or go to a support group that helps people in the same or similar position to see that you are not alone with your feelings. Holding them in may cause you to mentally implode, and you will cause yourself to become sick, lose sleep, or maybe lose your job from lack of focus or possibly exhibiting increased anger at the workplace.

Dr. Joni: The best words of wisdom that I heard are that you have to choose to be hopeless or you can be hopeful.

"The heart cannot be broken. The heart can be wounded so it seems the whole universe is a place of incredible suffering. But the capacity of the heart to endure suffering is unlimited."
—Henry Miller, author

Some people hide themselves in their work. Others may turn to alcohol or drugs to get by. These are temporary diversions from your reality. Instead, try to focus on that which you CAN control and expand on them. Your capacity for love can be manifested to a higher level if you come to a place of peace within yourself and choose not to be a victim of the pain and fear that you have. In other words, it is OK to feel these things, but don't let them own you; you can choose to gather the strength that we know you have, be our Love Warrior, and be the best friend and lover that you can be during the rough times.

Live in the present moment and go day by day, or moment to moment if you need to, in order to cope with the overwhelming feelings inside you. Our best advice is to seek out a therapist or support group where you can talk to other people who are going down the same path, and you can express yourself in a safe place. Remember, take care of yourself.

Dr. Joni: Unless your friends have had similar experiences, sometimes they may back away due to their own feelings of fear and helplessness. I lost some friends during these times and realized that true friends can still be there for you if they are able to put aside their own inner fears and still support you. We all remain friends, and now we are facing the realities of aging and dying parents. But, I will never feel alone again, and I know that I can make lemonade. Thanks, Nana!

Maintaining intimacy may become very difficult during these times. If your partner is able, try to cuddle, hold hands, and maintain physical touch. Hopefully, she will understand that you may need sexual release even if she has no interest. So maybe she can hold you while you masturbate or lend a helping hand. Depending on her abilities, it may spark some sexual interest in her too.

Try to make yourself feel better by becoming more grateful for what you do have together and what you have done together, and gather your mementos to look through together. Give yourself extra pampering too. Most of all, try to forgive yourself **and** your partner because no one wished this upon either of you.

Sometimes the malady can be chronic, and your partner may never recuperate back to the person that she once was. Some partners cannot handle this permanent feeling of helplessness or hopelessness. Before you walk out, please seek out therapy. There are often options that therapists know about and will help you with. You may be eligible for home health care, which will give you a break and some head space that is free from the hurts inside of you. Sometimes, you may need to force yourself to go out alone to social situations to keep connected to the healthy world. Or, take yourself to a movie to cheer yourself up. You may love your partner immensely, but your first responsibility is to yourself.

You need to keep your attitude up so that you can stay strong for yourself and your partner. It sucks to have to go out without your other half, but life is short, and you have to make yourself realize that we get only one time to ride this roller coaster of life, so try to enjoy the ride as much as you can.

You do not have to become a housebound martyr unless you choose it. Bring in a day nurse for a few hours to give you a chance to go out. If you physically can't handle the healthcare aspect of your partner's situation, then you may need to consider a full-time person, sending your partner to an adult day care facility, or ultimately nursing home care. But, then, your partner will be completely shut in to whatever facility she is in, and that is not a pretty situation in most cases.

You and your partner need to have deep, serious conversations about what is best for both of you so that you or she does not have resentment or regrets later. The sacrifices that are being made can destroy any romantic thoughts that you may have felt and will destroy the relationship if resentment starts to rule over love. Instead, try to intensify the love and romance as much as possible and your relationship can survive. It may even make you closer than before!

In some cases, depending on the nature of the illness or physical challenge, decisions about your relationship may need to be made. If you decide as a couple that the sexual component of your relationship is over, due to one person's inability to participate, remember that you owe it to yourself to maintain your own sexual health. Solo cultivation, or masturbation, is normal, healthy, and vital to your overall well-being and sanity. There is no shame in making sure that you maintain a sexual relationship with yourself. If your partner could no longer exercise with you, would you give up on working out? We don't think so, and there is no reason to give up on sexual release either. Taking care of yourself and your health from all aspects will make you stronger and give you the strength you need to be a supportive and loving partner.

You can bring food into a hospital most of the time and make a picnic on the bed. You can read love stories or old cards that you may have kept from each other. Bring in pictures of trips that you have taken together and family pictures to reinforce the legacy that you have made together and the fact that you are still alive. Hold hands, brush your loved one's hair, pamper the relationship, and reinforce it. Creativity is the tool to everyone's mental and physical survival. Sex can even be possible if you try positions that can work within your limitations. Obviously, unless you have a private hospital room, this may not be happening. Please consult with a sex therapist or marriage counselor to find out what you can do sexually that will meet both of your needs.

Sometimes you and your partner may be facing hardships together. The loss of a child, loved one, or a close mutual friend is tough because you are both feeling needs to be nurtured at the same time. It is easy during these times for people to push away the one person who loves them rather than to embrace the love between you. This withdrawal is caused by the overwhelming sense of loss, and they feel the need to turn away from everyone and everything. Again, if the romance is dwindling, try to do what you can and then seek professional grief therapy if needed.

No relationship can be hot and romantic every week of the year. Sometimes life gets too complicated. But, don't stress out or quit, and don't allow the romance to drift so far away that it can't be recovered. Maybe next week will be better! Keep your thoughts and actions positive, and keep the lines of communication between you open. A strong relationship will last through the test of time! Fight for it! That's what makes a Love Warrior!

CHAPTER 24.
Riding Off Into The Sunset Together

By the time you reach this section, it is our hope that you are well on your way to experimenting with new techniques and pleasuring your beautiful, intimate, erotic friend and partner in life. The whole point of this manual is not only to make you a better lover (that is a given), but also to make you a better partner and, in turn, a more fulfilled person. One of the wonderful things about women is that we generally think long term—when we say I do, I'm staying, or I love you and I mean it, we mean that. Unless one of you really screws up, you have a partner for life. The challenge is to make that life one worth living, channeling all of your energy into creating the kind of romance that most people only read about. You have already started to do that by reading this book, which has hopefully given you a new way to communicate verbally, physically, emotionally, and sexually with your mate. The secret is to make that last a lifetime. Please, embrace your sexuality and encourage your partner to do so as well. Laugh together, play together, and remake and rebuild the love that you have for each other, and celebrate that love on a daily basis.

Our point is this: The time has come to take your life seriously and place the most important things first. Your health and your relationship are the most important things in your world, and to preserve them takes work and attention. To enrich them takes dedication and a commitment to making each other happy. Do things together—take dancing lessons, play games, entertain more, travel more, go to the movies like a couple of kids and make out in the back row. Remind her that she is your fantasy, and do your best to be hers. Do things that make life worth living. Love is about more than sex, and passion is not only about how you make love but about how you live your life. This is our wish for you: live life passionately. Imbibe everything you do with passion, and your world will transform before your eyes. Live your life as if each day might be your last, and never forget to tell the important people in your life that you love them and why you love them because you never know if you will have another opportunity to mention it. Pay attention because the Universe is watching. When you live with more passion, amazing things will begin to happen, and miracles will unfold naturally. Take our word for it and go forth, my friend, because every amazing journey begins with the first step. Take it, and a whole new world will be yours. Remember that everything worth doing is worth doing to the best of your ability. Seize the day and seize the moment; otherwise, that moment will pass on by and be lost to you forever.

Our Parting Words and Best Advice: Kiss her like you want to kiss her every minute for the rest of your life, make love like you never have before, with your eyes and your heart wide open, and dance like no one is watching.

"Being deeply loved by someone gives you strength,
while loving someone deeply gives you courage."
–Lao Tzu, philosopher

APPENDIX I.
Ingredients to Avoid In Your Personal Products

Many commercially available personal products, such as shampoos, lubricants and topical sexual stimulants, have hidden ingredients that are harmful. That's why we endorse using natural and organic products for your sexual pleasure whenever possible!

Ingredients That Should Be Avoided:

- **Parabens**
- **DEA**
- **Glycerin**
- **Menthol**
- **Aluminum Sulphate**

PARABENS:

Parabens are a group of chemicals widely used as preservatives in the cosmetic and pharmaceutical industries. These compounds, and their salts, are used primarily for their bacteriocidal and fungicidal properties. They can be found in shampoos, commercial moisturizers, shaving gels, personal lubricants, topical/parenteral pharmaceuticals, spray tanning solution and toothpaste. Published studies have shown that parabens are able to be absorbed through the skin and to bind to the body's estrogen receptors, where they can encourage breast cancer cell growth. Parabens can mimic the hormone estrogen, which is known to play a role in the development of breast cancers. These preservatives are used in many cosmetics and some foods to increase their shelf life. A number of researchers and skin care experts have discovered that this preservative normally found in skin care products such as shampoos, moisturizers, shaving creams, and lotions can be toxic. It becomes even more dangerous the longer the person is exposed to it.

Parabens can do the following:

- Alter the estrogen processes among women, increasing the tendency of developing estrogen-dependent diseases like breast tumors.
- Heighten the existing allergic reactions experienced by the user.
- Decrease the sperm cell count among males.
- Promote skin allergic reactions like contact dermatitis and rosacea.
- Spur the development of skin cancer.
- Cause problems to fetal development for pregnant women.

Products without parabens are considered less toxic. Some of the better paraben-free products may contain the following problem ingredients to also watch out for:

DEA

Diethanolamine is a chemical that is used as a wetting agent in shampoos, lotions, creams, and other cosmetics. DEA is used widely because it provides a rich lather in shampoos and keeps a favorable consistency in lotions and creams. DEA by itself is not harmful but while sitting on store shelves or in your cabinet at home, DEA can react with other ingredients in the cosmetic formula to form an extremely potent carcinogen called nitrosodiethanolamine (NDEA). NDEA is readily absorbed through the skin and has been linked with stomach, esophagus, liver, and bladder cancers. A safer and more natural choice is cocamide DEA, or cocamide diethanolamine, a diethanolamide made by reacting fatty acids in coconut oils with diethanolamine.

GLYCERINE

Used for sweetening and preserving food, in the manufacture of cosmetics, perfumes, inks, and certain glues and cements, as a solvent and automobile antifreeze, and in medicine in suppositories and skin emollients. Glycerine in internal products has been linked to yeast infections. Glycerin is a close relative of glucose, otherwise known as sugar. When used in small amounts, a woman who is not prone to yeast infections will most likely experience no problems with using a nonwarming glycerin-based lubricant. However, if a woman is prone to yeast infections, inserting glycerin into the vagina gives the resident yeast extra food, creating an overgrowth of yeast that results in itching and irritation. Also, glycerine in a lubricant causes it to get sticky and tacky, which is no fun in the middle of sex!

MENTHOL

The majority of menthol in personal products is synthetic. Synthetic menthol comes in the form of l-menthol crystals that are derived from the plant's essential oil. Synthetic menthol can be irritating and drying to a woman's clitoris and vagina. A safe and natural choice is Mentha Pepperita, which is natural Japanese peppermint oil.

ALUMINUM SULPHATE

Also known as alum and used in many tightening products and also for pickling. This compound has astringent properties which causes the vaginal tissues to dehydrate. There is also a concern that aluminum may cause toxicity in the long run. There is some information linking products containing alum to possibly contributing to Alzheimer's disease. A safe and natural choice is capsicum, derived naturally from the pepper plant. This extract causes the vaginal walls to temporarily contract naturally with no negative long-term effects.

PHTHALATES

When it comes to making choices for sex toys, there is another health concern to be aware of. Phthalates have been proven to be carcinogenic over time, and they can be found in cheaply made toys that have a jelly-like consistency. Be sure to read all packaging or look for notations that the toys you buy are phthalate free. (All of the toys available on our store site are phthalate free!)

LATEX

About 30 percent of the population has a latex allergy, and the severity of it varies from person to person. Consider your partner's possible latex sensitivity when choosing safer sex products, such as condoms, dental dams, and rubber gloves. All three have latex-free alternatives that are commercially available.

APPENDIX II
A Store for Love Warriors:
www.LoveHerRightStore.com

To our dear readers,

Esther and I have a vision that incorporates our giving accurate information about sexuality and sexual practices, and we had a huge epiphany during the process. With so many products, toys, etc. available, shopping in a brick-and-mortar store is very intimidating, even for the strongest of us. How do you know what to buy? Do you feel comfortable asking the sales staff questions that make you uncomfortable? How do you know if you are buying products that are safe and body friendly? Because of my medical background and our experiences with too many loved ones contracting cancer from substances that are hidden behind scientific wording, we decided to take on another task. We chose to build an online shopping site. It is complete with lingerie, seduction products, spa and massage products, and an assortment of intimacy products, including toys, games, lubricants and topical stimulants, and instructional books and DVD's. We have personally inspected, tried and approved all of them and we gave them the big thumbs up!

We are constantly adding products to the site that we feel will aid in your quest to add spice to your love life and broaden your erotic horizons. Our pride and joy is to provide the best of the products available in order to make shopping a simpler, more approachable experience. We are also committed to making sure that your new passionate existence won't break the bank, so we have included items in all categories for every budget. These products are all from the highest quality sources and researched by us to keep our Love Warriors happy, sexy, and healthy!

If you find something lacking or you are looking for something specific that isn't listed, please email us at info@LoveHerRight.com and we will do the research for you! Love Her Right is more than a book—it's a movement!

Wishing You Love and Passion–
Dr. Joni Frater and Esther Lastique

RECOMMENDED READING LIST

While we have read well over a hundred books in conducting our research, there are a few that truly stand out as sources of great insight. The books listed here are our favorites that deal with love, relationships, and life. Check them out and share them with those you love.

Aronson, B.C., ed. (2007) *Love—Quotes and Passages from the Heart.* New York: Random House

Baxter, Leon Scott (2006) *A Labor with Love.* US: Lulu Publishing

Berman, Dr. Laura (2008) *Real Sex for Real Women.* London, New York: DK

Bierman, Dr. Jim (2007) *Of Sound Mind To Marry—A Reality Check from the Marriage Counselor for Pre-Weds.* US: Praeger Publishers

Blue, Violet (2002) *The Ultimate Guide to Cunnilingus.* California: Cleis Press

Brown, Douglas (2008) *Just Do It.* New York: Crown Publishers

Canfield, Jack (2005) *The Success Principles.* New York: Harper Collins

Chandler, Rebecca (2000) *The Clitoral Truth.* New York: Seven Stories Press

Chia, Mantak, et al. (2000) *The Multi-Orgasmic Couple.* New York: Harper Collins

Chia, Mantak, and Douglas Abrams (1996) *The Multi-Orgasmic Man.* New York: Harper Collins

Chia, Mantak, and Rachel Carlton Abrams, MD (2005) *The Multi-Orgasmic Woman.* US: Rodale

Deeter, Faith, MFT (2008) *The Conflict Pattern Revealed.* California: Lustre Publishing

Donaldson, Corey (2009) *Don't You Dare Get Divorced Until You Read This!* E-book available at www.TheFreedomAcademy.com

Eker, T. Harv (2005) *Secrets of the Millionaire Mind.* New York: Harper Collins

Erickson, Dr. Beth (2008) *Marriage Isn't for Sissies: Seven Simple Keys to Unlocking the Best Part of Your Life!* Texas: Marocom

Hopkins, Martha and Randal Lockridge (2007) *The New Inter Courses—An Aphrodisiac Cookbook.* US: Terrace Publishing

Katz, Elliot (2009) *Being The Strong Man A Woman Wants.* Canada: Awards Press

Kar, Jim. (2007) *If Food is Love...Cooking is Foreplay.* US: Xlibris

Kuchinskas, Susan (2009) *The Chemistry of Connection.* California: New Harbinger Publications

Lewis, Dr. Karen Gail (2009) *Why Don't You Understand? A Gender Relationship Dictionary.* US: Dog Ear Publishing

Love, Dr. Patricia and Jo Robinson (1995) *Hot Monogamy.* New York: Plume Publishing

Maria, Sarah (2009) *Love Your Body, Love Your Life.* Massachusetts: Adams Media

Matthews, David M. (2008) *Every Man Sees You Naked.* Arizona: Wheatmark

McCarthy, Barry W. and Michael E. Metz (2008) *Men's Sexual Health.* New York: Routledge

Poulter, Stephan, PhD. (2009) *Your Ex Factor: Overcome Heartbreak and Build a Better Life.* New York: Prometheus

Recommended Reading List

Sansone-Braff, Cindi (2008) *Grant Me a Higher Love*. South Carolina: BookSurge

Sausville, Peg. *The Truth About How to Kiss Women*. E-book available at www.kissingandmore.com

Zagata, Barbara *Attracting the Love You Desire*. E-book available at www.barbarazagata.com

Zagata, Barbara (2008) *Don't Stress-Manifest*. US: Booklocker.com

CPSIA information can be obtained at www.ICGtesting.com
Printed in the USA
LVOW120036261011

252100LV00002B/7/P